ID0952676

sexy
little numbers

HOW TO GROW YOUR
BUSINESS USING THE DATA YOU
ALREADY HAVE

DIMITRI MAEX
WITH PAUL B. BROWN

sexy

little numbers

WITHDRAWN

CROWN BUSINESS / NEW YORK

Published in the United States by Crown Business, an imprint of the
Crown Publishing Group, a division of Random House, Inc., New York.
www.crownpublishing.com

CROWN BUSINESS is a trademark and CROWN and the Rising Sun
colophon are registered trademarks of Random House, Inc.

Crown Business books are available at special discounts for bulk
purchases for sales promotions or corporate use. Special editions,
including personalized covers, excerpts of existing books, or books with
corporate logos, can be created in large quantities for special needs. For
more information, contact Premium Sales at (212) 572–2232 or e-mail
specialmarkets@randomhouse.com.

Library of Congress Cataloging-in-Publication Data
Maex, Dimitri.
   Sexy little numbers : how to grow your business using the data you
already have / Dimitri Maex with Paul B. Brown.—1st ed.
      p. cm.
   Includes index.
   1. Consumer behavior—Research.   2. Marketing Research.
3. Advertising—Research.   4. Data mining.   I. Brown, Paul B.
II. Title.
   HF5415.32.M34 2012
   658.8'3—dc23   2011043275

ISBN 978-0-307-88834-1

eISBN 978-0-307-88836-5

Printed in the United States of America

Book design by Elina D. Nudelman
Illustrations by Chris Udemezue
Jacket design by Whitney Cookman

10 9 8 7 6 5 4 3 2 1
First Edition

FOR KATHERINE, RAY, AND BRUCE

CONTENTS

CONTENTS

sexy
little numbers

WHY NUMBERS HAVE ALWAYS BEEN SEXY

Ads that follow shoppers around as they go from one website to another; precise, real-time updates on the effectiveness of your marketing campaigns; and the ability to target the absolutely most profitable individuals within your customer base—these are just three of the thousands of things possible today, thanks to analytics, *the shorthand description of the art and science of analyzing all the data that is out there.*

So, you might think numbers have just suddenly become sexy; but that's far from the case.

It's probably fair to assume that our sexy little numbers started to pop up in marketing after the invention of the first direct-response campaigns. Aaron Montgomery Ward invented the mail-order catalog in 1872, and Richard Sears and Alvah Roebuck copied it in 1886. While there is no real evidence of how these early catalog pioneers measured their success and optimized operations, they had the ability to do so; and the fact that both catalogs thrived for more than one hundred years (to be replaced by their online equivalents) suggests they probably did a good job at it.

Indeed, Claude Hopkins's *Scientific Advertising* (1923), a forerunner of this book, states: "The time has come when advertising has in some hands reached the status of a science. It is based on fixed principles and is reasonably exact. The causes and effects have been analyzed until they are well understood. The correct methods of procedure have been proved and established. We know what is most effective, and we act on basic laws."

Hopkins and later John Caples, in *Tested Advertising Methods* (1932), wrote mainly about mail-order and other direct-response vehicles. It was easy for them. They knew to whom they sent their catalogs, or direct mail pieces; all they had to do was track whether those people actually ended up buying. That worked fine until mass media—radio and then television—came along. There was no simple way to tell who, precisely, heard or watched a broadcast. New techniques would be required for these new media to maintain the same levels of marketing accountability.

The first applications of more advanced mathematical techniques began in the 1950s, when operations research and management science models that had become popular in production and manufacturing following World War II were applied to marketing for the first time. Although extremely primitive by today's standards—when we know exactly how long someone looked at an online ad, which parts he clicked on, and what actions, if any, were taken as a result—the models began to provide an understanding of the marketing and media mix on outcomes such as brand awareness, consideration, and, ultimately, sales and profit.

The third era in the evolution of analytics happened during the 1990s, when customer relationship management (CRM) became an obsession for many marketers. The possibilities offered by new, powerful databases transformed direct marketing—and our sexy little numbers along with it—and it is easy to see why. In his 1996 book, *The Loyalty Effect*, Frederick Reichheld showed that a 5 percent improvement in customer retention rates usually yields a 25 percent to 100 percent increase in profits. That same year, Garth Hallberg's *All Consumers Are Not Created Equal* appeared, in which he demonstrated (as we will talk about in Chapter 2) that a small proportion of a company's customers usually represents a disproportionate share of revenue. As a result of these findings, companies vowed to get to know their most valuable customers. They introduced loyalty cards that allowed firms to capture transactional data and they invested heavily in data-warehousing technology that stored all customer information in one database. Lifetime value models predicted what a customer would be worth over the long haul, and anti-attrition models were built to predict an individual's likelihood of ceasing to be an active consumer. The CRM revolution expanded marketing effectiveness tools and techniques considerably, and an analyst's ability to sort through vast quantities of data was soon tested on customer-centric data derived from digital media.

With digital communications—anything sent over the web—everything is measurable. Everything generates data, and the volumes are enormous. Google's digital database, which is probably the largest, captures more than 1 *billion* searches per day worldwide. This huge quantity of data can give companies unprecedented visibility into how customers engage with brands and how that engagement ultimately leads to revenue.

E-commerce environments provide us with a closed-loop system, which, in marketing effectiveness terms, gets us close to nirvana. We know which media individuals have been exposed to, how they came to a specific website, and what they do once they arrive there. We can observe these individuals' entire shopping behavior, all the way to their actual conversion to a sale.

Digital data is also available in real time. We no longer have to wait weeks or months to learn the impact of our marketing activities. We can get a read almost instantaneously, allowing for immediate optimization. Digital has put the marketing math revolution on steroids.

Sam Palmisano, CEO of IBM at the time, explained the new world better than anyone during a speech to the Council on Foreign Relations in 2008 in which he pointed out that "all things are becoming intelligent: New computing models can handle the proliferation of end-user devices, sensors, and actuators and connect them with back-end systems. Combined with advanced analytics, those supercomputers can turn mountains of data into intelligence that can be translated into action, making our systems, processes, and infrastructures more efficient, more productive and responsive—in a word, smarter."

Take Zara, the flagship brand of the Spanish retail group Inditex SA, as an example. By integrating analytics into every single part of its business, it has done what was thought to be impossible in the clothing industry—going from the design table to stores in a matter of weeks. It is not uncommon for other retailers to be working nine to twelve months out on their line of clothing for Christmas.

What does all this mean for you and me personally? As a result of analytics and the interconnectivity that Palmisano was talking about, picture your refrigerator in the very near future: Not only will it tell you when you are running out of milk and butter, but it will be able to draw up a shopping list and actually send the order to your local supermarket, which will then deliver it to you.

BUT WHAT ABOUT PRIVACY?

All of this is pretty wonderful, but it comes with a price. Some people are concerned about marketers being able to collect all this data about what they buy and where they go online.

I am going to talk a lot about privacy in the last chapter, but let me touch on it here, and my position may surprise you. I believe people are rebelling for valid reasons against widespread data collection for commercial purposes. Data collection is largely unregulated and hidden. And that is wrong.

But things are changing. In the absence of other standards, and because consumers have told us, quite rightly, that they have concerns, the advertising and marketing industries have begun to regulate themselves. We have pledged that we will not collect personal identifiable information (PII) without the consent of the consumer, and we give the consumer the opportunity to opt out of any data collection, but we will also educate consumers about our reasons for collecting this information in the first place.

I am hoping that education will help people understand that what may seem like an intrusion at first is, in fact, to their benefit. I know that sounds Orwellian, but consider how few people outside of the marketing profession understand that advertising is needed in order to fund the creation of content, especially in an age when people expect more and better free content. Consumers have demonstrated again and again that they will not pay full freight for the content they enjoy, whether it is to watch their favorite television show or to spend time on their favorite websites. Without advertising, most websites would be behind a pay wall, you would have to pay a subscription fee to see them, and every television channel would be premium.

To keep most of that content free, advertising-supported

media isn't going away, but we now have the ability to make it less of a nuisance. Let's say you are a twenty-five-year-old gamer, and the TV networks need to expose you to six minutes of advertising to pay for the production of your favorite thirty-minute show. Would you rather have six minutes of advertising about the latest games or six minutes of general advertising? Most gamers would prefer the first scenario, but for that to happen you need to let math marketers in on your tastes, habits, and preferences, so they know enough to send you commercials relevant to you.

And if you do that, you might actually see fewer commercials. Ads that are personalized provide a better return for the advertiser, and advertisers will therefore pay more for a personalized thirty-second ad, or an online banner ad, than for a general one. That means you could see fewer ads, but the content providers will receive more money for them. Sounds like a good deal all the way around.

That's yet another potential benefit of all these sexy little numbers that are out there.

With that by way of background, let's get to work.

CHAPTER ONE

HOW THIS BOOK WILL HELP YOU GROW YOUR BUSINESS

I work in an industry known for reducing complicated ideas to a single thought. These tag lines—"Merrill Lynch is bullish on America," "I think, therefore IBM," and "Don't Leave Home Without It"—were all created by my colleagues at Ogilvy & Mather.

And in my corner of the ad agency—I recently ran Ogilvy's analytics team but now lead the New York office for Ogilvy One, our direct digital marketing division—we operate on a single premise: The most successful companies today are those that are able to convert the "data deluge" we all face into insights that drive real growth.

Our job is to help our clients uncover those insights. To do that, we need to explain what we discover within their data in simple, straightforward terms. (While the CFO is probably comfortable when I talk about "logistic regressions," the rest of the people in the C suite usually don't speak math shorthand, and their eyes glaze over after ten or fifteen seconds when I do.* So, I have learned to present my ideas the way the "creatives" do, in simple, hopefully memorable images such as

---

*Recently, one of the guys on my team came to me all excited about a presentation he'd just seen. "This company was cool, man," he said. "They appended three thousand variables from a third-party data aggregator to the ad server cookies, ran a CHAID tree to score them on likelihood to convert, and fed the scoring algorithms back to the ad servers in SQL so they could use them for targeting individual cookies on ad exchanges." He was right, this was exciting stuff. But I doubt that most readers would get the same kick out of this that he did—at least, not the way he explained it.

"At sixty miles an hour, the loudest noise in this Rolls-Royce comes from the electric clock." (That was another one of ours.) And I will try as much as possible to use this type of language in this book.

Simple language only enhances this powerful fact: There is now a proven way to increase dramatically both your company's sales *and* its ROI *using data you probably already have but may not be aware of.*

How?

Well, if you think about it, there are really only two sides to every business: supply and demand. The supply side, how a company is going to fill orders—i.e., how they will fulfill their customers' needs—is the one that a business controls. The company heads know, for example, how much productivity will increase if they buy a new machine.

The supply side is where most left-brainers—the logical, financial types—feel comfortable. For decades, they have increased the efficiencies of supply chains, streamlined processes, and developed measurements to track progress.

The demand side, on the other hand, is something companies don't control; consumers do. Sure, you can try all kinds of things to reach customers, but ultimately it is the customer/consumer/client who decides if he is interested in what you have to offer. The demand side is the fuzzy place where cause and effect are not always clear. Did he buy because the product was perfect for his needs, because he liked your ad, because your price was appealing, because of word-of-mouth—or was it some combination of those factors and a hundred more?

Here finding out what happens when you turn the dials and push the buttons is a messy business. The customer bought immediately after clicking on your Internet ad; but was the banner ad the reason she bought? Figuring it all out is what I do on a daily basis. As you will see, I use the clean, tried-and-tested tools from the supply side and apply them to the messy demand side of the business.

These tools can help you, in the words of the book's subtitle, grow your business in a way that increases both your sales and profits.

This is not only vitally important to those of you in the C suite—after all, the shareholders ultimately will judge you on how effectively you deploy their money—but to employees at all levels of the company. Marketers and people who run business units need to know which are the most profitable customers to target; researchers must have a (profitable) consumer in mind as they set off to create new products or services; those in customer service want to pay the most attention to the firm's most valuable users/buyers; and, of course, the people in finance will always ask whether the company is going to make any money on its latest undertaking. By employing the ideas we are about to talk about, the return on your investment can be huge.

How huge? Here are two quick examples using the techniques I will be sharing with you:

- Caesars improved their return on online advertising spending by 15 percent to 30 percent by analyzing data generated from customer reviews about the hotels the company owned. There are software programs that not only search out every comment customers make on the web, but automatically sort those comments into scores of categories, and the company used those findings to change their offers and the language in their ads. For example, customers raved about the views from the hotel, and now those views are featured prominently in Caesars ads, while the price of the room is given less prominence.

- TD Ameritrade increased new account openings by 14 percent from the company website just by making very small changes to the copy, design, and images on the site, based on an incredibly thorough examination of its home page. Our team at Ogilvy tested every single word, color, and design element with customers to see what could be improved. It turned out that simply changing the signup language from "Apply online now" to "Get started" and altering the color of the button customers clicked from orange to green made a dramatic difference in the number of people who opened accounts.

As these examples show, the material in this book is not theoretical. It is already being used by companies to increase demand for their products. I am going to show you how you can do the same thing.

By looking differently at the *existing* data you have about your customers, you can improve:

Your strategy. You'll learn how to fine-tune your overarching approach to both your customers and the competition based on the insights the numbers about your business can provide. For example, you will discover who your most profitable customers are, who is most likely to buy from you, and which customer segments are not worth targeting.

The tactics you use to carry out your strategy. Your data, when viewed correctly, will tell you how to approach and sell to your most profitable customers and the best ways to reach those who are likely to buy more from you.

The execution of your tactics. Your data will help you pinpoint where you will get the biggest returns and when would be the best time to implement your tactics.

There are two simple reasons why these improvements

are possible: First, remarkable breakthroughs in technology allow us to sort through all the data about customer behavior to find discernible—and predictable—buying patterns. We have always had the data; but until now, companies could use it only in the crudest terms. Second, just about everything we do today generates data, giving us a much more complete picture of the people who do business with us, and the potential revenue companies are missing, as the following story shows.

On a recent business trip, I woke up in the Canary Wharf section of London and checked out of the Hilton. I took the subway to Paddington Station. From there, I hopped on the Heathrow Express, supposedly the most expensive train in the world, but still cheaper and faster than a cab (and it doesn't make me carsick).

I checked in for my British Airways flight to JFK airport. Before boarding, I stopped at Boots, the largest drugstore in the UK, to get a four-pack of cucumber wet wipes. My wife, who is British, tells me they are the best in the world and she cannot find them in the United States (like Marmite and Cadbury Creme Eggs, this is another strange product British expats miss when living abroad). I also browsed the perfume section, where a saleswoman complimented me on buying Gucci's latest fragrance, Flora. Three hours after waking up, I boarded my plane home.

In this short period of time, I left behind a rich trail of data. Hilton, if it knew where to look, would have seen it was my third stay in that hotel within six months. They also could have discovered I like a glass of wine before I go to bed and that I prefer the continental breakfast despite a promotion for the full English one. The London Transport Authority, if it wanted to, could see I was in town for a week—I had purchased a seven-day pass—and that I had crisscrossed the city during the day, always to go back to Canary Wharf in the evening. They might also have noticed that seven years ago, when I lived in London, I did the same thing every day.

The people who run the very expensive Heathrow Express now have buried somewhere in their records that I used their services for the third time in six months. British Airways would have noticed the same. Boots could have figured out that I was probably another British expat (well, Belgian with a British wife, actually) hamstering their fabulous cucumber wet wipes. And Gucci, had it been paying attention, would have noticed I bought the fragrance in a store with a couple of big video-screen monitors advertising it nonstop.

All this data was being gathered without my even going online to surf the web. If I had, then companies would have been able to track my every click, even if I didn't purchase from them.

The point is not to tell you how much I travel for business, but to give you a tiny example of the volumes of data that are being collected and hardly used. Sure, Hilton knows (if they look) that I have a frequent-stayer account (Hilton HHonors), but I have yet to receive a targeted email or letter that says, "The next time you are London, Mr. Maex, may we suggest . . ." (some hotels have started to do these kinds of mailings). Boots has never mailed a catalog to our Brooklyn apartment, and I have never received a solicitation from Gucci, which is probably a good thing, given how much my wife likes their products.

While I was traveling, millions of others were generating similar volumes of data that same morning. They, like me, do this through interacting with websites, social networks, mobile devices, cash registers, etc.

Companies haven't been using the vast majority of information we generate because—up until now—it has been too difficult to get at it in a useful way. I sympathize. The volume of data gathered every day is staggering. To put the amount into perspective: Imagine a database holding all words ever spoken by human beings since the beginning of time. Now, if you were to take 200 of those databases, you would have just about enough storage to hold all the data that will exist by the end of 2012. That's a lot of data and the numbers will only increase dramatically in the years ahead.

But companies no longer have the excuse that the data is too hard to sort through. The tools invented in the last few years make it remarkably easy.

Let's see how. Here's a real-life example involving strategy. The story begins right after my wedding.

CISCO SYSTEMS: A CASE STUDY

Katherine and I chose the most romantic destination for our honeymoon: Silicon Valley. It wasn't exactly what we had planned.

A couple of days before we got married, in 2004, I got a call about a job opening in San Jose. While I love my native land of Belgium, I'd always wanted to work in the United States. You need big volumes of information to make my job fun. There are only ten million people in Belgium, so the databases are small. This was a great opportunity to work where the markets have bigger scale and are more sophisticated.

So, right after Katherine and I got married in Antwerp's beautiful sixteenth-century town square, we found ourselves in the center of Silicon Valley with all of our stuff in boxes. My job would be working with Cisco Systems, the forty-billion-dollar technology company.

Cisco's new head of demand generation had asked Ogilvy

for help in setting up what they were calling an "advanced analytics" group. The goal of this new unit would be to figure out precisely to whom Cisco should be marketing and how much they should invest to reach those people. Up until this point at Cisco—and maybe at your company as well—these decisions were made by gut feel backed by some, often anecdotal, data.

That might be fine for a start-up company, but when you are an established firm, one spending a lot of money on marketing—hundreds of millions of dollars a year, in Cisco's case—you need to do better than hunches and one-size-fits-all rules of thumb, such as you should spend 5 percent of revenues on marketing.

So Ogilvy sent me to Silicon Valley to see if I could help Cisco. Apart from their head of demand generation, nobody else at the company was necessarily waiting for the creation of an advanced analytics group. Marketers in general weren't particularly interested in analytics back then. Most people didn't go into marketing because they liked math; quite the opposite. So I had some convincing to do. Especially since the person who asked me to set this up, the only advocate I could count on, had left Cisco to join Oracle by the time I landed in San Jose!

So there I was in my little gray cubicle (the concept of a cubicle was foreign to me; I had seen it only in movies like *Clerks*, where the people who inhabited them always seemed to have dead-end jobs), on my first day at a new job in a new country. No one was asking for my help. No one really understood what advanced analytics was for. Heck, they didn't even know what the term meant.

Given all this, the first thing I did was to look for buddies, like-minded people who understood the potential power of data and analytics in marketing. One of them was Mike Foley, who was in charge of Cisco's marketing database. He could tell me all about the information Cisco had on their customers and prospects. This was great. If I was going to set up an advanced analytics function, I would need data. Data is the raw material for everything I do.

Mike and I teamed up, and I started to delve into the data, familiarizing myself with everything Cisco knew about its customers—which was a lot. For every company that had ever bought a Cisco product, there was data on when the companies bought, what they bought, how much they spent, and how often they bought from Cisco. (You probably have—or can get your hands on—this kind of data, too. Someone, or some department, in your company is sending out invoices. The data is probably inside their computers.)

Mike and I got really excited about this kind of information, but I realized no one else in Cisco's marketing organization would. And why should they? These were just raw numbers. We needed to demonstrate how the data could help Cisco's marketers make better decisions. The key to doing that is keeping things simple. You need to tell a story with the data. Numbers alone don't convince anyone of anything.

So I started to play around with the data, trying to find a way to paint a picture that would refine Cisco's marketing strategy. I ended up using a very simple framework that had been around at Ogilvy for a while. It's called the Value Spectrum Model, and it maps customers on a two-by-two grid like the one on page 16.

I will go into this in detail in Chapter 3. But for now, all you need to know is that this is a simple segmenting exercise that divides your customers into four categories based on how valuable they are to you. It tells you at a glance with whom you should be spending time and which customers are safe to ignore. When we did it for Cisco, it looked like this:

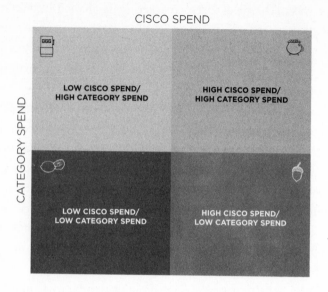

CISCO SPEND

CATEGORY SPEND

LOW CISCO SPEND/
HIGH CATEGORY SPEND

HIGH CISCO SPEND/
HIGH CATEGORY SPEND

LOW CISCO SPEND/
LOW CATEGORY SPEND

HIGH CISCO SPEND/
LOW CATEGORY SPEND

SEARCHING FOR BILLIONS MORE IN SALES

So far, so good. And if you have done similar segmentation exercises, this kind of matrix will look familiar to you. But here is the difference between what you may have done in the past, and what is possible today: Before, you couldn't do much more than sort your customers into the four buckets at a conceptual level. Sure, you might, for example, have a handle on your top twenty-five customers. And you might even have a "sense" of your next fifty, but you couldn't identify them exactly. However, while you might know that you have thousands of dependable (read: repeat) customers in the Northeast, you could not single out Mary Smith—or where to find her (123 Main Street, Plymouth, MA)—or how to reach Ms. Smith directly (781–555–1234; MarySmith@email.com). Cisco certainly couldn't. This has changed now. You can use the techniques described later in this book not only to segment your customers, but also to identify them individually (something Cisco now does routinely).

And you can go even further. While you already have information (somewhere) about how much your customers are spending with you, for Cisco we developed a statistical model that showed how much its customers were spending with competitors as well. That's no small thing. If you know you already have the vast majority of your customers' budget, you don't want to keep spending money trying to get them to buy more. They simply don't have much more money to spend and you would be wasting your marketing dollars. Conversely, if you know that you have only 10 percent of your customers' wallet, you can be fairly aggressive in going after the other 90 percent.

Here's how we figured out what Cisco's customers were spending with others. Let's say there are two architecture companies in Chicago, each with 25 employees and with similar revenues. We know from our database that A&A Partners spends $50,000 a year on IT, all of it with Cisco. Our records also show that B&B Partners does business with Cisco, spending $10,000 a year. Now, Cisco does not know exactly what B&B Partners spends on IT. But they do know that they have almost the exact same profile as their competitors over at A&A. This means that Cisco can be relatively confident that B&B is spending $40,000 of its $50,000-a-year IT budget with someone other than Cisco—and it is worth going after B&B for that remaining $40,000.

The statistical models we built do a very similar assessment on a much larger scale, across millions of companies globally. These models allowed us to identify the "Jackpots" in the Value Spectrum framework and learn about what they bought, how much they bought, when they bought, what inducements got them to buy, what other products they bought with their purchase—the list is virtually endless.

Still, you need a way to present the data so it is easily understood. I have built a lot of very complex segmentation frameworks for clients to help them determine who are their potentially most profitable customers (and we will discuss some of them later in this book), but I often come back to the good old Value Spectrum, with its Jackpots, Nuggets, and the like. When the data is presented this way, the conclusions are obvious, and marketers know immediately how to use it.

Mike loved the framework. He immediately understood that the simple story presented by the two-by-two matrix could demonstrate the power of the databases he had been building over the years for Cisco.

This wasn't just some theoretical exercise. We had actually tied it to his database so that if a salesperson wanted a list of Jackpots in greater Detroit, we could actually pull the list of companies with the names and contact details of the decision makers. Simple but powerful stuff.

Working through channels, we got permission to present what we had to the sales force. At the end of my speech, someone asked, as a joke, "I don't suppose you can give me the names of those Jackpots." That's when we handed them lists of Jackpots and Nuggets by their sales territory. They were thrilled.

Having the sales force on board got us the attention of the marketing community within Cisco. I was asked to present to James Richardson, then Cisco's global CMO. Now, that was a very big stage, and we needed to prove that the two-by-two matrix worked. Clearly, it was too early to see the sales force's success with the idea, so we went back and looked at historical data. To keep things manageable, we singled out a specific segment of Cisco's market—small and medium businesses (SMBs)—and tracked changes in their buying behaviors over time. (For example, a customer who was a Golden Nugget might become a Jackpot; a customer who was an Acorn could become a Nugget. You get the idea.)

The migration matrix below shows the number of companies that moved from one segment to another and the revenue associated with the change.

FY 04/05

FY 02/03

					0	TOTAL
	8,705	2,640	200	31	2,833	14,409
	2,767	3,369	446	104	7,660	14,346
	188	494	5,301	1,839	3,465	11,287
	25	92	1,632	2,303	7,299	11,351
0	4,940	9,618	5,274	8,991	692,829	721,652
Total	16,625	16,213	12,853	13,268	714,086	773,045

FY 04/05

FY 02/03

					0	TOTAL
	28,231,119	-86,311,374	-876,566	-747,962	-75,968,611	-35,673,394
	10,308,480	-859,266	11,689,854	-37,751	-11,420,133	109,681,185
	287,400	-12,467,497	11,752,737	-54,199,522	-82,802,880	-137,429,762
	736,250	-1,611	66,666,187	230,044	-10,911,497	56,719,372
0	91,830,565	13,508,956	194,258,103	11,886,436	0	411,484,060
Total	31,393,815	-86,130,792	283,490,315	-42,886,755	-181,103,121	404,781,461

While the table above captured in one place all the movement that had occurred, it was not intuitively obvious what had happened. In other words, I didn't have a clear story to tell. So we simplified the numbers in the table to show both the good and the bad and you can see that in the table on page 20.

TOP 5 POSITIVE REVENUE STREAMS

0 → 🌰 $194m - 5,274 companies

0 → ⚱️ $192m - 4,940 companies

⚱️ → ⚱️ $128m - 8,705 companies

▯ → ⚱️ $110m - 2,767 companies

🥜 → 🌰 $67m - 1,632 companies

TOP 5 NEGATIVE REVENUE STREAMS

⚱️ → ▯ -$86m - 2,640 companies

🌰 → 0 -$83m - 3,465 companies

⚱️ → 0 -$76m - 2,833 companies

🌰 → 🥜 -$54m - 1,839 companies

🌰 → ▯ -$12m - 494 companies

0 represents noncustomers

With this method, people could quickly see not only that
the company had grown revenue in the small and medium
business space by $404 million from fiscal year 2002/2003
to fiscal year 2004/2005, but specifically where that growth

came from. But the analysis also gave Cisco a very accurate picture of where the company was losing revenue.

That was better than the fairly detailed table you saw on the previous page. But it wasn't good enough. You don't want to wait until your boss—or the shareholders—say, "Well, what does it all mean?" You want the story to be as clear as possible.

So, before I went to talk to James Richardson, I boiled down everything I had learned (I will show you the process I used a bit later in the book) to the following three recommendations (which would be backed up by the two charts you just saw):

1. *We need to get more from our existing customers.* On average, gaining an additional 1 percent of a Nugget's IT budget means an annual increase of $8.6 million in revenues. Obtaining 1 percent more of an Acorn's spending means a gain of $6.3 million a year.

2. *We must convert more Jackpots to Nuggets.* For every 1 percent of Jackpots we can turn into Nuggets, revenue on average will climb by $5.7 million.

3. *We need to stop Nuggets from migrating downward.* For every 1 percent drop in sales to a Nugget, overall revenue falls $4.1 million a year.

Distilled to this level of specificity, we had a really interesting story to tell, one that could have a profound effect on how Cisco thought about marketing in general. Up until then, the role of marketing had been to generate awareness and consideration of the Cisco brand and create leads for the sales force to close.

Doing the three things I suggested would not only make the company much more customer-centric, it would allow Cisco to concentrate its marketing assets in the places that would generate the highest possible return.

Armed with all this information, I headed off to Building 10 at Cisco. That's where John Chambers, Chairman and CEO, and all the senior executives like James Richardson are located—the inner sanctum. It was a big deal. You don't get to present to the global CMO of a company like Cisco every day. I remember having a discussion with Heather, the person who headed the Cisco account for Ogilvy, about whether we should include the table with all the numbers cited on page 20 in the presentation. Heather didn't think it was a good idea. She thought it had too much detail for someone as busy as James. I really wanted to include it because, although it has a lot of numbers, they were numbers representing real money. And not only did it tell a story, it also allowed us to show how granular we could get in showing where James was winning and losing money. In the end, Heather told me not to include it, but I sneaked it into the presentation anyway. It was James's favorite slide. We will talk about data visualization later in the book; for now, the takeaway point is, do not be shy about showing the actual numbers if they tell a story.

The presentation to James gave us the exposure we needed to really get traction. It was clear to everyone how advanced analytics could uncover insights that could change the strategic direction of marketing.

Cisco adopted our recommendations wholeheartedly. They moved from marketing efforts focused primarily on generating leads, to creating programs designed to get more revenues from existing customers.

We didn't stop with the Value Spectrum, though. Mike and I spent the next six months building propensity models for every product in Cisco's portfolio. Propensity models calculate the likelihood of either an existing customer or prospect purchasing a particular product during the next twelve months. This allowed us to identify which product would be the next logical purchase for every individual company and deploy our sales efforts accordingly.

How did we do this? Through a process called "look-alike modeling," which is exactly what it sounds like. Let's say you notice that once your global export customers hit $5 million in revenues, they tend to buy IP telephony systems (since those systems dramatically reduce the cost of international calls). Knowing that, you go to all your global exporting customers who are approaching $5 million in sales and start—as Cisco did—pitching them IP telephony systems. Our propensity modeling doubled the response rate Cisco got to its emails trying to interest potential customers in its products—and the whole purpose of those emails is to generate leads. The company was very happy.

As you can see from the Cisco example, the idea of using existing data about your customers is not some hypothetical idea. Everyone from Ameritrade to UPS—and scores of far smaller companies as well—has launched programs to do this as a way to increase sales dramatically at virtually no cost. It has started to alter forever the way we think about the information we have captured about our customers, in addition to changing the way we think about ways to increase ROI.

But this was something our agency's founder, David Ogilvy, probably could have predicted. One day he was talking about one of his greatest laments. In typical Ogilvy fashion, his comment was clever and contained a telling truth.

"I admit that research is often misused by agencies and their clients. They have a way of using it to prove they are right. They use research as a drunkard uses a lamppost—not for illumination but for support."

We now have the ability to turn on the light.

A Quick Look at the Road Ahead

I have structured *Sexy Little Numbers* in the way most companies do business, addressing the key questions managers and leaders have to answer when it comes to figuring out how to use their data more effectively.

For example, you need to begin by asking, "What are you trying to do?" (After all, if you don't know where you want to go, any road can take you there.)

Before you start to look at your data differently, you need to know where you are, and what you want to accomplish. Is your goal more sales? Greater customer loyalty? What exactly are you trying to achieve? Where are the opportunities and the upside?

Once you know, you can then determine how your data can help you.

To show you how this could play out in practice, meet the extremely fictional Sue Smith, senior vice president of marketing at the equally fictional Planetary Co. She has come to me for help, and her overall objective is clear.

"My boss, the COO, has made my goal for this year simple," she told me. "I need to increase sales 4 percent more than growth in GDP, without any increase in my budget." (This kind of objective is typical.)

Here is the kind of conversation Sue and I might have in response to her goals.

DIMITRI: Once you know your objectives, the first step is to figure out who you should be trying to sell to. [Or, as in Chapter 2, "Who Should You Talk To?"] All customers are *not* created equal. You want to target those that matter most. Here, it is all about the importance of segmentation and the various techniques we will explore in detail—things such as ranking customers based on lifetime value, or frequency of purchase, or whatever criteria (and you can have more than one) are important to you.

SUE: OK, I see. Well, to be honest we haven't done much in the way of segmentation. I can probably tell you who our twenty most important customers are. But I don't think I have a list written down anywhere. As for the other things—well, our approach there has been fairly haphazard as well.

DIMITRI: No problem. Here are some of the things you will need to answer, and I guarantee you already have data that can help:

- *How do you determine your target audience?* That is, how do you know who are your most valuable customers or prospects?

- *Are you going to look just at revenue?* Or do you also want to take into account the share of your target's wallet you have captured?

- *Do you know how to calculate share of wallet?* If not, I can show you.

- *Do you know whether your best customers are preparing to defect to the competition?* Again, we have techniques that will show you.

- *Do you know how much your best customers will be worth if they stay with you over the course of their lifetime?* Yes, we can help you figure that as well.

Once you know to whom you want to talk, you'll need to know what to talk to them about [our subject matter in Chapter 3]. Here our focus will be all about what I call creating a value exchange. Amazon.com is probably the classic example of a company that does this well. As a consumer, I am more than willing to have the company track my purchasing behavior, because I know in return I am going to get recommendations tailored for me.

SUE: We have never thought about creating a value exchange. What are the sorts of questions we would have to ask?

DIMITRI: Here's a partial list:

- *Do you really understand what your customers are looking for?* If not, how are you currently tailoring their communications?

- *Have you done any research into the needs and attitudes of your target audience?* If not, what are the best ways we can use qualitative and quantitative research techniques to get a better understanding of your customers?

- *How can we take the insights from this research further and create archetypes of consumers?* Soccer Moms are an archetype; so are Metrosexuals—and it helps to have a vivid image in mind when we try to communicate with our customers and potential customers.

- *Can we go even further and predict what specific products or services individuals will be most interested in?* I'll give you a hint: We can, by looking at their *current* purchasing behavior.

- *How can we learn even more about our customers through text mining and even neuroscience?* All of this can help us be more relevant to our customers and dramatically increase the return on marketing investment.

Don't worry if you don't know the answers. We can use the existing data you have, and supplement it with the use of outside vendors to come up with solutions to all these questions.

SUE: OK. By this point, I am going to know what kind of customers I want to talk to, and what we want to talk to them about. But how do I find these people?

DIMITRI: Great question. And, not surprisingly, answering it is the next step in the process [see Chapter 4]. As you know, there has been a fundamental shift in the way we identify potential targets. We used to make sure we advertised where we knew large groups of potential customers would be. We'd buy space in the newspaper we knew they read—e.g., the *Los Angeles Times*—or on a television show we knew they watched—let's say, *The Simpsons.* Sure, not everyone we reached was a potential customer, but that "waste" was just a part of doing business.

Now we have the ability to target individuals. For example, a "cookie" on someone's personal computer can tell us she went from CNN.com to a website that provides information about new cars and, once there, she spent a great deal of time researching hybrids. Knowing that, Toyota can make sure that person—and that person alone—sees a banner ad for their Prius the next time that person logs on to CNN.com.

Again, it is all about asking (and answering) the right questions so we can find the right prospects, once they have been defined. Here are some of the questions we will want to find answers to:

- *How can we figure out what media to use to reach our customers?*

- *Should we target different geographies differently?* If so, how detailed do we get? Do we differentiate between states and zip codes? And what media do we target geographically—only traditional media such as outdoor and print or also digital media?

- *How good are we at finding customers through search engines such as Google?* Have we optimized our digital assets to ensure maximum return from search engines?

- *Do we target different individuals differently?* If so, do we do this through databases we build ourselves from the transactional systems we have internally? Or do we buy files from outside vendors?

SUE: This all sounds great—and expensive. As I said, I am operating in the real world. I don't have unlimited funds; in fact, I don't have one extra dollar to spend.

DIMITRI: Understood. That's why the next step in the process is figuring out not only what you need to spend, but how to spend it more efficiently. We do that by asking:

- *How much are you spending now on creating demand?*

- *How did you determine your budget?* Did you use common sense or simple rules of thumb, or do you use a more scientific approach such as econometric modeling— something, I promise, I will help you understand the inner workings of.

- *Can we and should we use a hybrid approach that combines the principles of science with decision-making methodologies?*

- *What did you spend during the recession?* Do you need advice about how to set budgets in the context of changing macroeconomic conditions?

- *How long-term a view do you take with your marketing investments?*

Now, once we understand how you set your budget, we need to understand how you spend it. So, we need to talk about how you:

- align your investments with your main marketing tasks.
- allocate your budgets by geographic regions.
- allocate your budgets by medium.

What we really want to do is get an idea of how you arrived at your overall marketing mix. I will show you how to identify ways to make the entire process more fact based and scientific. We are not trying to eliminate creativity, just augment it.

SUE: What do we need to do to determine if we are on the right track?

DIMITRI: Ah. We just got to one of my favorite topics: execution, making sure we are doing the right things right. The first step in doing that, of course, is to understand how well your efforts are working—more specifically, what is working and what isn't [Chapter 6]. We can do that by asking:

- *How do you measure success?*

- *What metrics do you use and how did you arrive at them?* We can help you determine the right metrics so that you measure only what matters.

- *Do you measure inputs, outputs, and outcomes?* If not, we show you where to find the data that will allow you do that.

- *What tools can you use to measure across different platforms?* Not only do you need different tools for different media—search versus print, for example—but within the categories, you want to use different tools as well. With online, for instance, how you measure the effectiveness of email could be different from how to chart the response to banner ads you buy.

- *Do you use dashboards?* And are they designed in the right way?

- *What other data-visualization techniques do you use?*

- *How do you attribute the success to individual marketing activities?* Is it rules-based, or do you use more accurate multivariate statistical techniques (don't worry if you don't know what that means; it is not as scary as it sounds).

Once you know what is working, you can increase the money put behind the efforts that are showing the biggest return—obtaining that funding by cutting back on what isn't working well, as opposed to asking for a budget increase. How do you do more of what works and less of what doesn't? It's all about optimization [Chapter 7]. You improve your efforts through analysis and testing.

- *Are you currently learning from what works best?* Do you have a process in place for consistently measuring, analyzing, and optimizing?

- *How do you use the insights into what works and what doesn't to become more creative in how you go to market?*

- *Do you test?* If so, do you have a process that rigorously tracks responses so that you know what to change and what to keep?

- *Do you take full advantage of the possibilities of testing digital platforms?*

Testing is not a one-off process. For example, in the TD Ameritrade case we mentioned earlier in this chapter, we ran 243 slightly different home pages to determine exactly what text to use, what visuals to display, how to organize the page, and what colors to employ in order to get the highest number of visitors to become TD Ameritrade customers.

SUE: OK. I understand the process. Let's go.

DIMITRI: Terrific. Let's begin by talking about which people you need to talk to in order to have all those sexy little numbers you have at your disposal work for you.

CHAPTER TWO

TARGETING: WHO SHOULD YOU TALK TO?

It is only customers, of course, who can supply the increase in sales (and profits) you are looking for. But the question is: which customers? Who do you target; who should you talk to?

My answer: You always want to fish where the biggest fish are. And the sexy little numbers you have (or can easily get) can be your best fishing rod.

In this chapter we will talk about how you identify the customers who are—or have the potential to be—the most valuable to you.

We will first lay out some very simple things you can do to find those customers and we will progress to the point where you can know with near certainty who is going to leave you and who will turn out to be a customer for life (and what he or she will be worth to you as a result).

I started my career in Brussels—not necessarily an advantage for an aspiring analyst, because the Belgian market is very small. There are fewer than 11 million people in my country. (By way of comparison, the state of Ohio alone has 800,000 more people—and it is only the eighth most populous state.) This means that the advantages of using analytics in Belgium are limited.

However, Belgium does have a couple of things going for it. Great food (Belgium has the most Michelin stars per capita) and, of course, great beers. This makes it a popular destination for people who enjoy the good things in life.

Garth Hallberg, one of the few people with extensive experience in both direct and mass-market advertising, is definitely one of those people. When I first met Garth in Brussels, he had already had an illustrious career at J. Walter Thompson, where he was in charge of the huge Unilever account (in 2010, Unilever spent 6 *billion* euros on advertising). He was a famous marketer and a great strategist. But Garth also loves numbers. He likes nothing better than playing around with spreadsheets. And though he wasn't really a statistician by trade—he was trained as a journalist—he was a master at telling stories with numbers.

One of his early stories demonstrated how the Pareto principle applied almost uncannily to marketing. In the early twentieth century, Italian economist Vilfredo Pareto observed that 80 percent of the land was owned by 20 percent of the people. Garth extended the concept to marketing firms, where he proved that, for many brands, 80 percent of the profit is generated by only 20 percent of the customers. (What naturally follows from that is that you want to treat those customers extremely well.)

Garth illustrated his findings with the little triangle below that describes a particular product.

SPEND IN THE CATEGORY

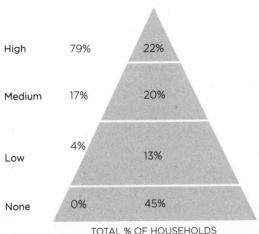

High	79%	22%
Medium	17%	20%
Low	4%	13%
None	0%	45%

TOTAL % OF HOUSEHOLDS

The triangle was a very intuitive illustration of the principle. For example, as you can see, just 22 percent of the households accounts for 79 percent of this product's sales. Not surprisingly, this easy-to-understand approach caught on. Garth trademarked the Differential Marketing pyramid and wrote a book about it called *All Consumers Are Not Created Equal.* It became an instant best seller that helped spark the customer relationship management (CRM) revolution of the 1990s.

I worked with Garth in Brussels on his next big idea. This time his hypothesis was that there is a correlation between the degree to which consumers feel "emotional loyalty" toward a brand and how much they spend on it. We set out to prove this hypothesis by sorting through the BrandZ database.

It was no small task. BrandZ is the world's largest brand database. Through it, we have access to insights from 1.5 million customers, in 31 countries, who have given their opinion about 50,000 products and services in 380 categories. As you can see, it was a huge amount of data.

Garth needed a young number cruncher to help him mine this huge database and decided on me. (I still think it had more to do with his love for the restaurants on the Rue des Bouchers in Brussels than with my quaint skills.)

The great thing about using BrandZ data was that it had already sorted customers by how appealing they found a particular brand. You can see that by looking at the BrandZ Emotional Loyalty Pyramid you see on page 33.

The levels of the pyramid are both sequential and mutually exclusive. Customers must satisfy all the requirements for each step before they can climb to the next, and they can only exist on one level. (You can't be on the "advantage" and "bonding" steps simultaneously, for example.)

BRANDZ Emotional Loyalty Pyramid

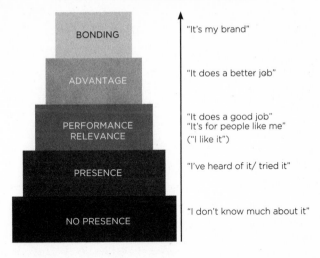

The pyramid gave us the perfect data about the levels of emotional loyalty a consumer had with a brand. All we needed to do was correlate this data with what we knew the responders to the BrandZ survey spent.

As I went through the analysis, I would go to Garth with numbers and insights. He would always ask me, "What's the story, Dimitri?" and he would say, "Keep it simple." He really taught me the power of simplifying the complex. The questions when you are working with data are always: How can I turn these numbers into insights and, more important, how can I communicate these insights in an intuitive way to non-technical audiences?

The result of the project was five universal truths we were able to prove across thousands of brands across the world. These findings should be valid for your company's products and services as well.

1. *The greater the emotional loyalty, the greater the value of a customer.*
   Value leaps dramatically when bonding (the highest level of

emotional loyalty) is achieved. To pick just one example: In Italy's insurance sector, a bonded customer is worth four times the value of an average customer; in France, a high-value bonded coffee customer is worth twenty times more than an average customer. This just makes sense. A person who will drink only Starbucks—going out of her way to find one of their shops, or to buy the brand in her supermarket—is worth substantially more to Starbucks than someone who really doesn't care what kind of coffee she consumes.

2. *Bonding is a key driver of brand leadership.* The margin of leadership is often additional sales contributed by bonded brand buyers. In France, bonded customers account for 90 percent of the difference in market share between the top two coffee brands.

3. *Bonding is the only level of emotional loyalty that significantly reduces attrition or increases retention.*

4. *Not surprisingly, bonding is extremely difficult to achieve.* Few consumers reach this stage. In Italy, for example, only 2 percent of insurance customers are bonded.

5. *All bonded consumers are not created equal.* The bonded high-category buyers produce far greater value than the bonded medium-category users.

The fact that high-value bonded customers are worth twenty times more than an average customer is remarkable and illustrates that a very small proportion of customers can make or break a company. This is why prioritizing who to talk to is so crucial.

No one in marketing understands this better than direct marketers. They have been using the "Fish where the big fish are" philosophy for decades. This helps them focus their limited marketing dollars on the few customers who really matter. And when it comes to direct marketing, perhaps it is no surprise that no one does it better than the world's post offices.

Since direct mail represents such an important part of their revenue—think of all the catalogs and credit card offers you receive—they are always at the forefront of making the direct-mail channel as effective as possible. This requires them to be masters at direct marketing themselves. For example, to demonstrate how quickly they could deliver packages, one European postal service I worked with sent fresh flowers to thousands of direct-marketing prospects they were trying to reach. And it is common when they have a new initiative—such as providing a discount to mass mailers who sort their offerings by the zip code of the receiver before dropping them at the post office—to target different individuals within a company differently. The CFO might get a pitch that focuses on how presorting the mail will save him money on shipping costs, while marketers will be told presorting will get their message to recipients faster.

Post offices did for mail what Google has done for search and online display marketing: Be the best at it and demonstrate that if done well, the channel can be extremely effective. And how better to illustrate this then with a post office itself?

The Stamps and Collectibles (S&C) division of a postal service designs, produces, and markets stamps and related products. Their core audience is collectors, and their challenge is obvious. Stamp collecting, which was never exciting to begin with, is becoming less relevant. The hobby has an increasingly old-fashioned image, and the existing collectors are getting older—and fewer and fewer people are coming up the ranks to replace them.

S&C has always been a very profitable and important revenue stream for postal services. Stamp collecting may account for less than 5 percent of their revenue, but it can return double-digit profits, which is easy to understand. Hobbyists buy the stamps but never use them, putting them in their collections instead. The stamps the S&C sells them represent virtually pure profit. If there ever were a segment you'd want to grow, this would be it.

The majority of the stamps are bought (fittingly enough) by mail, and so the postal service has in its database not only the names of the purchasers, but also what they bought. Every name. Every transaction. This data allowed us very quickly to draw up one of Garth's pyramids, which showed that, say, 4 percent of the native population accounted for 71 percent of the total S&C revenue.

But who should the S&C target for growth? Not all of those 4 percent were equal. So we wouldn't want to blanket all of them. Some were vastly more profitable, and since we are going to target individuals, we might as well focus our efforts on the few philatelists who really made the difference.

Besides, that was not the only place growth could come from. We might be able to convert good customers into great ones. To figure out who to go after, we employed the Value Spectrum. It works exactly as it did when we talked briefly in Chapter 1 about how I employed it for Cisco.

Let's look at this framework in detail since it is one of the most simple and elegant yet powerful segmentation models still around.

Value Spectrum

The Value Spectrum is a method for segmentation that allocates customers to categories based on their total market value. It enables you to find out how much they are going to spend in your product category—and what their loyalty is to your particular products; i.e., how much of what they are going to spend will go to your company. That concept is usually known as "share of spend" or "share of wallet." It doesn't really matter what you call it. It's how much of the customer's money he decides to give to you, when it comes to his purchases in the category where you compete. If a customer spends $200,000 on computers, and he buys $45,000 worth of those computers from you, you have a 22.5 percent share of his wallet.

As you can see from the two-by-two matrix that makes up the Value Spectrum Model, customers fall into one of four segments.

VALUE SPECTRUM MODEL®

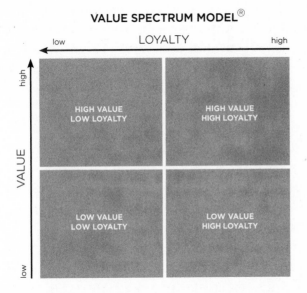

Why is this useful? Well, as the four quadrants show, creating a Value Spectrum underscores the need for treating different kinds of customers differently. Since the value and loyalty of the customer aren't the same in each segment, what you spend on him needs to vary as well. Obviously, you want to spend the most time and attention on the customers who can provide you the highest returns.

So, as you can see, you can use the Value Spectrum to allocate sales and marketing resources and to develop differential marketing strategies (by focusing on where the biggest opportunities are).

Let's go through each segment as if we were working with S&C's entire customer base.

High Value/High Loyalty. Customers in the upper-right quadrant (both high-value—i.e., they spend a lot of money in the category—and loyal to your brand) are "Nuggets" (as in solid gold). They are the core customers of any company. Like the actual gold nuggets themselves, these customers are hard to find, relatively small in number, and extremely valuable.

Your key objective here is retention—both in terms of keeping these customers *and* maintaining their level of purchases. Despite their high degree of loyalty, some customers in this group will have the tendency to decrease the amount of money they spend with you—due to budget cuts, for example, or because they were attracted by a competitor's offer. Given their loyalty, this happens less here than in the other groups, but even small losses among this group can produce a substantial negative impact on sales and earnings because of their disproportionate contribution to your business.

High Value/Low Loyalty. Customers in the upper-left quadrant (who spend a lot of money but have low loyalty to your brand) are what I call "Jackpots," because they have the *potential* to really pay off. In fact, they are the group with the highest potential.

There is often a real battle for these customers, since Jackpots are often the Nuggets of your competitors. They are loyal to someone else but they spend a lot in the category; so if you win them over, the gains are substantial.

Low Value/High Loyalty. Customers in the lower-right quadrant (who are low-value, but highly loyal) are "Acorns." If nurtured, you can reasonably expect their purchases from you to grow. They know about and are loyal to your offerings, so two major hurdles have been vaulted. But they are simply not buying enough from you today. Your goal should be maintaining their loyalty and, if possible, increasing the size of their wallet, i.e., the amount of money they spend in the category. This can sometimes be done by educating them about the category. This objective is most attainable in categories with a high "elasticity of demand," such as most foods and beverages. There, purchasing levels are determined by personal preference ("I think I'll have bottled water instead of a soft drink") rather than by circumstances ("I need enough detergent to do five wash loads a week"). Thus, sales can be increased by changing usage or consumption habits in addition to taking business from a competitor.

Low Value/Low Loyalty. The last group is of small interest to you. They contribute little to current sales and offer little future potential, yet companies who don't go through this Value Spectrum exercise often spend just as much on these customers as on their most valuable ones. That's why identifying this segment is so important. It allows you to shift the money you are spending on this relatively unimportant group to where it can do you more good. As a result, your marketing efforts become much more effective—*without spending any more money.*

If you implement this segmentation framework for S&C, you would focus communications on the few customers who mattered. They would start getting "exclusive offers" and bigger discounts on products. In short, you would do everything you could think of to make them feel special (because they are).

The results would be phenomenal. You could imagine sales

increasing in the neighborhood of five times for campaigns that used our segmentation frameworks; and, for every $1 invested in these new communication efforts, we could get $4 back. Analyses like this on behalf of small clients drew the attention of the folks who were running the biggest account in the London office at the time—British Telecom (BT).

BT: SHARE OF WALLET

Now we were starting to talk scale! Telecom companies have enormous amounts of information about their subscribers. Every call you make generates data and gives the phone companies the ability to gain insights into how valuable a customer you are, and what your potential could be, in this highly contested market. Any information that a company can gain about its share of wallet is vital, especially in phone markets, such as landlines, which are not growing. The business-to-business arm of British Telecom, BT Business (BTB), had been successful in holding onto existing customers through loyalty and discount programs. It was clear they were able to keep customers, once they found them. They "simply" had to find them, and we set out to examine the data to enable them to do that very thing.

We started by looking at the spending patterns of people who used BTB exclusively for their phone service and discovered that what a customer spends on telephone service depends on:

1. *The total number of lines a company has.* No surprise there. The more phone lines, the more calls an organization is likely to make.

2. *What business sector they are in.* Obviously some kinds of businesses—such as shipping companies—do more business on the phone than others.

3. *Geographical dispersion of a company (whether it is a multi- or single-site company).* It makes intuitive sense that companies with more than one location spend more time on the phone. They're talking to their colleagues in other locations as well as to customers.

For a very high proportion of its database, BTB had the data in these three critical areas. We used it to build a "peer to peer" comparison algorithm that enables you to compare apples to apples. It doesn't make a lot of sense to compare the revenue potential of a two-person consulting firm to what can be generated by an international call center. We needed a way to compare companies in the same industry to see where the biggest opportunities were.

So we first calculated "the spend"—what the monthly bill was for each customer per phone line. Then we sorted all of BTB's customers, from high- to low-spend per line. Now we knew how much each customer was spending, not only in total but also by phone line. For example, we knew Business A, a car-rental company with 40 separate phone lines, was spending $3,000 a month with BTB, or $75 per line.

Then we compared Business A to all car-rental companies in our system, to see how it measured up. Because there can be regional differences, we compared it to all car-rental companies nearby—say, all the car companies in the Cornwall area. Let's say that the top 5 percent (in terms of spend per line) of car-rental companies in and around Cornwall spend, on average, $120 per line with BTB. We would then assume, because they are the top spenders, that these companies spend all of their money in the category with BTB; i.e., BTB had 100 percent share of their wallet. And because we know that spend is driven by geography and sector, we can assume that Business A would also spend $120 per line. The fact that we have only

$75 of their business means that they must be spending an extra $45 with competitors.

This meant that company A was spending a significant portion of its phone budget with someone else, and it would be worthwhile targeting them.

To make sure our algorithm was correct, we checked it three ways. We looked at data from directory assistance, call spikes, and third parties. Let me explain what we did.

Directory-assistance data. On average, similar companies place about the same number of calls to directory assistance. For the sake of argument, let's say it is 1 percent of the total calls placed. If my company makes 1,000 calls a day and 10 of them are to directory assistance, it is a pretty good bet the BT has close to 100 percent of my telephone business, if the averages hold true. But if BT, who owns the directory assistance, sees that a company that is making 100 calls a day to directory assistance is making only 1,000 calls a day through BT, the telephone company could be fairly sure the firm was making a total of 10,000 calls daily—9,000 of them with someone else. That would be a client BT should target.

Call-spike data. Many customers rented a telephone line from BT, but had a box installed that routed their calls through a different carrier. If the box breaks down, all calls go through BT, resulting in a spike in the company's BT spend. That allows BT to see the customer's true total call volume. The bigger the spike, the smaller BT's share of wallet. Again, our model confirmed this trend.

Third-party data. You never want to rely exclusively on someone else's research, but it can help you double-check your work. In this case, it confirmed our assumptions about what non-BT customers were spending on phone service.

This validation gave BT the confidence to use the algorithm for targeting. The takeaway: This relatively straightforward modeling exercise gave BT a solid estimate of the total call volume for every company in its database. It allowed British Telecom to use potential revenue (Company X spent a lot of money on phone service, but very little, or none, with BT) as a targeting criterion.

BT SEGMENTATION

The success of this share-of-wallet exercise got us to the next step: a presentation on how to build BT Business's entire segmentation strategy.

Of course, agencies like Ogilvy pitch for creative assignments all the time, but this was going to be a different animal. We were pitching data analytics work. Our senior managers—who knew that winning this project would open doors for even more business with BT—would have no choice but to put the geeks (like me) front and center, rather than the special creative teams who usually do these presentations.

They were nervous, and I was very nervous. First, I had to write just about all the material myself. Second, I had never participated in a pitch. English is not my native language; and while the head of the BT account had heard I was good with numbers, he wasn't sure whether this kid with the funny Flemish accent could actually write and then present in English.

But I had a pretty good idea of how we could help BT. There were two specific business issues their new segmentation needed to address.

First, it needed to address how to deal with the small and

|44|

medium-sized business markets. When it was a monopoly, BT never had a reason to segment its customers. People had no choice when it came to who would provide their phone service, so BT had no reason to single anyone out. Now it needed a clear segmentation strategy to deal with the small and medium business, or SMB, market.

BT's largest customers always had their own account manager who knew intimately what his clients needed. That would continue to be the case, but the company needed to develop an effective strategy for dealing with all other customers as well.

Second, it needed to figure out who to target when it came to "new wave" services such as broadband Internet, mobile, and ICT (information communication technology, including wireless and security). In the past, BT had looked only at call volume. But as the market evolved, BT diversified its product portfolio; it needed a new segmentation framework that took all these products into account.

In addressing these two business issues, BT looked for a segmentation strategy that:

- Defined the total SMB market, including not only customers but also prospects.
- Identified addressable needs where it could sell more "new wave" services.
- Enabled resources to be targeted accurately.
- Not only explained past purchasing/usage behavior but also predicted future behavior.

We proposed a multidimensional approach where businesses would be segmented based on hard factors, such as revenue, potential, and risk, on the one hand, and soft factors, such as business needs, on the other. The following table gives an overview of the approach:

DIMENSION	HARD	SOFT
COMPONENTS	Current value, risk, potential and sophistication	Business needs addressable by ICT solutions
WHAT IT DESCRIBES	How customers behave	Why customers behave the way they do
TARGET DECISION	Who we will target from a budgetary point of view?	Who we will target from a needs point of view?
MARKETING DECISION	Differential investment in customers	Personalized messaging

The hard segmentation prioritized the businesses BT wanted to target—those looking to grow their revenues. The soft segmentation enabled BT to personalize its communications based on the needs of each small and medium-sized business. We will focus on the details of the hard segmentation in this chapter and the soft segmentation in the next one. (Our focus in Chapter 3 will be on what to talk to potential customers about. We will discuss the way BT explained to small and medium business customers how they could grow their revenue and I will show how you can combine hard and soft segmentation to create an integrated approach.)

BT liked our approach and awarded us the business—and a very tight deadline. We immediately set off to determine what *value* really meant to the company. Value is different for everyone. For BT, value had four components, as you can see from the diagram on page 46: how much customers were spending with the company at the moment (Current Revenue); what was the likelihood they would remain a customer (Risk Propensity); how deep their relationship was with the company—i.e., were they buying just about everything BT had to offer (Intensity);

and how much of their category spend was going to someone else (Total Non-BT Revenue).

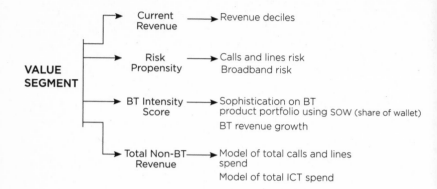

The first component, Current Revenue, was the easiest to calculate. BT needs to send out a bill to its customers every month. The bill shows exactly how much it is charging, so all we needed to do was go into the billing system and calculate the sum of all the charges a customer (a small business, in this case) had generated. It was a pretty straightforward exercise, and at the end of it BT would know who were the customers with the highest spend.

The second component, Risk Propensity, was harder. Once the market opened up, there was "churn" as customers left to join new competitors. Therefore, we had to try and predict the likelihood that a current client would leave BT by building a churn model based on information from ex-customers. If a lot of these previous customers came from a certain geographical area (because there was a very successful regional competitor, for example), then existing customers who lived in that region would get a higher churn score and have a greater potential to leave. If we saw that ex-customers tended to make more international calls (because competition focused on favorable international rates, for example), then customers who made a lot of international calls would get a higher churn score as well.

The model we built looked at data such as total call volume; call volume during certain times of the day and week; and the balance between local, regional, and international calls. It highlighted where clear differences existed between former customers and current customers. We used those variables to calculate the likelihood that a current customer would leave. Specifically, we ranked every existing customer in the BT database on a scale of 1 to 100. A customer ranked a 1 is almost definitely going to stay with you. One rated 100 is all but out the door. (Later in this chapter, we will explain how these churn models really work.)

In the third component, the BT Intensity Score, we were trying to capture the strength of the relationship a company had with BT. This was especially important at a time when BT was trying to reposition itself from a telephone-only provider to a full-scale integrated communications provider that offered not only telephony, but mobile networking solutions, data security, etc.

We came up with a very simple solution for this. We scored all BT products on a scale from 1 to 5, with 1 being very basic products like standard telephony and 5 being very advanced products like complicated network security solutions. Then we calculated, for every customer, what percentage of the customer's total spend with BT was spent on each product.

We used that percentage to calculate the weighted average of the complexity scores for every individual customer. That weighted average became the BT Intensity Score.

Let me walk you through the math in the table on page 48.

	PRODUCT INTENSITY SCORE	SPEND COMPANY		SPEND % COMPANY		INTENSITY SCORE COMPANY	
		A	B	A	B	A	B
Landlines	1	$100	$200	55.6%	90.9%	56	91
Internet	2	$50	$10	27.8%	27.8%	56	9
Wireless	4	$20	$10	11.1%	11.1%	44	18
Security	5	$10	$0	5.6%	5.6%	28	0
Total		$180	$220	100%	100%	183	118

As I said, we attributed a product intensity score to the various items BT sold. Landlines got a 1, as a basic service with relatively low margins; security products received a 5, because they were more complicated and carried higher margins.

Columns under the Spend heading across the top show what Companies A and B spend on each product, while columns under the Spend % heading show the percentage of their total spend per product. For example, Company A spends 55.6 percent of its telecommunications budget on landlines ($100/$180).

To get the intensity score for Company A, we multiply the product intensity score by the total Spend %. (For example the product intensity score of 2 for Internet times the 27.8 percent of total spend) and then add up all the numbers in the column. That gives us an overall product intensity score of 183 for Company A. For company B, we would multiply the Product Intensity Score by the Spend % to get the numbers in column 8. When we add up column 8 we see that Company B has an intensity score of 118. The higher the number, the more valuable the customer.

The final component was the share of the customer's wallet BT was *not* getting, calculated by the share-of-wallet exercise, described earlier, for every product and service BT offered. We complemented this number with industry research. For example, it was easy to obtain reports on total ICT spend for companies in specific market categories by size of company and their location. You always want to check to see if your model is right by using proven data.

Calculating the non-BT spend was very important because it enabled us to identify where the opportunity was for BT. To find out, we created a detailed Value Spectrum, basically a more elaborate model of the one I presented earlier. We found a strong correlation between total category spend and spending with BT. In other words, if you spent a lot of money on telephony, you were probably spending it with BT. That wasn't surprising. BT's monopoly had just ended and not a lot of people had yet switched to other providers. You would have seen the same situation in the United States in the early 1980s, just after the breakup of AT&T.

Once we calculated the four value components for every customer and prospect, it was time to combine them into one overall rating, so it would be possible to tell at a glance how valuable a customer was. This is always a good idea. The simpler you can make the data, the better.

We arrived at six value segments, displayed in the table on page 50. (Remember, "intensity" refers to how loyal they are to the BT brand.)

The insights from this new segmentation gave BT a completely new perspective on its marketplace. For example, we identified $6 billion of potential revenue in Segment 3. BT had never focused on this segment before, since they never took into account what their customers were spending with competitors. And, as you can see, they also identified 8,000 very-high-value customers whose spend was more than 10 times higher than that of the second-highest segment. This allowed BT to focus its efforts on keeping these very important customers in Segment 1.

	NUMBER OF CUSTOMERS	DESCRIPTIONS	SUGGESTED STRATEGY
SEGMENT 1	8,000	Very high concentrated opportunity, high intensity	Actively grow and retain personal service and bespoke solutions.
SEGMENT 2	172,000	High opportunity to increase revenues, high intensity	Grow and retain differential service and customer experience.
SEGMENT 3	364,000	High opportunity, medium revenue potential, low intensity	Acquire/cross sell, invest in education and changing perceptions of BT as telecommunications provider. Develop a "next step" selling approach. Invest in acquisition.
SEGMENT 4	151,000	High revenue (currently), low opportunity for growth, high intensity	Retain focus on loyalty, customer experience. Deliver best price, service and rewards for remaining loyal.
SEGMENT 5	319,000	Low opportunity, limited revenue, medium intensity	Manage for cash. Maximize profit by converting to low-cost channel maintenance where possible.
SEGMENT 6	477,000	Low opportunity, low opportunity for growth, low intensity	Maintain/low-cost acquisition. Approach as "acquisition" for new products and services with low cost-channels.

On the lower end of the scale, as you can see in the table, there are some very big segments with very limited revenue. This made it clear to BT that the company needed to come up with cost-effective ways to serve these large volumes of customers.

IF YOU DON'T HAVE THE DATA, YOU CAN PROBABLY CREATE IT

The BT case study is a great example of how you can mine all the data you have about your customers. And BT certainly had a lot of data. But what happens if you don't have this much information? This is often the case in the automobile industry. People buy a car once every few years. In between purchases, the car manufacturer can count itself lucky if customers go to see a local dealer for service; and, as cars have gotten better, the periods between required maintenance have gotten longer, reducing the number of those infrequent interactions even further.

In these situations, you can often rely on outside vendors as a starting point to gaining the specific information you need. Take a luxury carmaker, for example. How could they use data to increase the number of quality leads for new cars?

People who buy luxury cars are special. They are attracted to the brand they choose by its heritage or unique styling and dramatic performance. But given the fiercely competitive nature of the luxury automotive category, attracting the right kind of new customers is a continual challenge.

In solving the problem within a direct marketing context, there are a number of options. One option is to buy the mailing lists of companies that sold luxury products that appealed to people who also bought this company's cars, but these lists are typically too small. The company would need more names to achieve the sales volume required, but large compiled lists are simply too general to produce acceptable response and conversion rates. (We will discuss these types of data sources in Chapter 4.) The company could create its own list, of course. But you never want to reinvent the wheel. If they could figure out which people on those general lists were likely to buy their cars, they could use our criteria and purchase only the names that matched.

In working with a company like this, we would study the characteristics of current customers. We would likely find that they tended to live on either coast in upscale, suburban areas. Most of them would be older, at least in their late fifties, and often empty nesters. And then, much as we did for Cisco (see Chapter 1), we would build a statistical model to identify those households within the compiled lists that were most likely to become customers.

The benefits of this approach are twofold: First, it would provide the carmaker with a significantly greater universe of names to mail offers to; second, and more important, it would allow them to achieve a higher sales rate when compared to the more restricted and costly lists previously used.

This case clearly demonstrates how you can more effectively acquire new customers by analyzing the profile of your existing customers.

LIFETIME VALUE: THE ULTIMATE PREDICTION

The metric with the biggest potential payoff is lifetime value (LTV). If you are able to estimate what a current (or potential) customer will be worth to your organization over her lifetime, you know just how much you can invest in acquiring and growing that customer.

While the concept of lifetime value is pretty straightforward—it's how much someone will spend with you if you can turn him into a customer today and can keep him forever—the calculation is a bit more complex. The way the folks in finance put it, lifetime value is the discounted cash flow of a

the twelve months prior to March, Mary had a steady
n of 8 to 12 flights a month. In March she dropped to
hts. This is unusual for Mary; so, something seemed to
been different in March, for this one month only. She
have taken a month off, started working at home, or she
have fallen ill. Given her travel patterns, the chances
spending 80 percent less on airline travel over the next
e months are slim. There is a higher chance she might
20 percent in revenue, though, especially if she has two
ee more months of low activity.

tween last March and November, Susan's pattern was
similar to Mary's. However, starting in November, she
raveling less with our airline. There is something sys-
going on. This is why I gave her a higher likelihood of
less during the next twelve months than I did for Mary.
m seems to have a very different flight pattern—much
erratic. A drop to only two flights per month is not un-
on for Tom; he has had even bigger declines before. This
I am not sure at all if Tom will drop in revenue in the
welve months.

el sure that you scored Mary, Susan, and Tom similarly,
we all intuitively analyze patterns of behavior in the
way. We looked at how often these three frequent fliers
n average, how much variation there is on a monthly
how big the drop was in March, and whether that drop
en going on for a while.

an create a statistical algorithm that analyzes this infor-
n in a way that is similar to our thought patterns. All I
need to do is translate the factors we intuitively looked
mathematical variables. Here is how that would work:

customer's future revenue streams. In English, that means how much someone is going to spend with you over the course of his or her lifetime, adjusted for inflation.

Lifetime value is a function of three things:

1. *Current value:* What is the customer spending with you now?

2. *Future value growth or decline:* How much more or less will the person spend with you in the future?

3. *Length of the relationship:* Exactly how long will he or she be a customer?

The last component—the length of the relationship—is, of course, the hardest to calculate. You know—or can easily find out—what someone is currently spending with you. And a look at your records will reveal if that number has been rising or falling over time. But how long a customer will stay loyal to you is another matter. How do you know? Well, believe it or not, your data can tell you.

Let me show how by using a theoretical example I developed. Imagine that a major airline, let's call it Continent Air, asked me to help them make their customers more loyal. A big part of this task would be first identifying the customers most likely to leave. If they could be identified, the airline could develop programs to persuade them to stay.

Like every airline, Continent Air has tons of data. It knows when each customer flies, how often, in which class (first, business, or coach) and the destination. I would use a representative sample of the data to determine how to calculate a person's revenue at risk—how much of this customer's business might drop off.

I developed a formula that predicted that a person's revenue at risk is determined by:

- The customer's current value
- The probability the customer will decline in revenue
- The estimated percentage of the projected decline

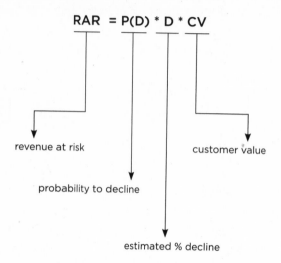

$$RAR = P(D) * D * CV$$

revenue at risk

probability to decline

estimated % decline

customer value

If you multiply these factors together, you get the person's revenue at risk (RAR).

The RAR concept, if explained accurately, could be extremely powerful and differentiating. I would have to come up with a way to get this across very quickly and clearly to a nontechnical audience. Specifically, I would have to answer a question like this: "How can a statistical model predict that someone is going to spend less money—and perhaps a lot less money—with us in the next couple of months?" This sounds like crystal ball, voodoo stuff.

But it really isn't. While algorithms are often perceived as magical formulas to be understood only by mathematicians, most of the time they simply mirror the way we naturally think.

To prove that's true, let's look at three people who are frequent fliers: Mary, Susan, and Tom. For reasons we don't

know, they all flew fewer times in Ma
to last. Mary flew three times this I
a year ago. For Susan it was one flig
two for Tom, as opposed to ten a yea

	MAR	APR	MAY	JUN	JUL	AUG	SEP	OCT	NOV
Mary	10	11	9	11	10	9	11	12	10
Susan	9	10	9	11	12	10	8	11	9
Tom	10	5	15	1	1	9	6	1	15

Take a close look at how often the
twelve months before this past March
table below. What do you think the
Susan, and Tom will drop their reven
percent, 50 percent, and 20 percent?

	DROP 80% IN REVENUE NEXT YEAR	DROP 50% REVENUE NE YEAR
Mary		
Susan		
Tom		

When we asked other people the sam
it relatively easy to answer. And their an
to and pointed in the same direction as

	DROP 80% IN REVENUE NEXT YEAR	DROP 50% IN REVENUE NEX YEAR
Mary	20%	30%
Susan	35%	45%
Tom	10%	10%

WHAT YOU AND I LOOK AT INTUITIVELY	VARIABLE IN MODEL
How often they fly on average	Average number of flights per month
How much variation there is month to month	Variance of monthly number of flights
How much the drop was in March	March volume minus average volume prior 12 months
How long had the drop been going on	Number of months with flights less than 30% of the average of the prior 12 months

The right-hand column contains the variables in the model that predict the likelihood that someone will drop in revenue. The statistical model would look at customers who actually dropped their revenue more than 20 percent, 50 percent. and 80 percent in the last year and look at what these predictive variables (more on this in a second) looked like in the twelve months before they started dropping off. This would teach the model how these predictive variables can be combined to calculate the likelihood that someone's spending will decline a certain percentage. Obviously, this is important information. If you know that one—or more—of your most important customers (in terms of revenues and especially income) is probably going to leave you, you can take steps to prevent it. You would talk to the customer, of course, to find out why she was thinking about leaving, and perhaps offer her incentives (discounts, upgrades, perks) to get her to stay.

Now, you and I looked at the data, and intuitively figured out who was likely to stop being a customer of the airline. But this is one place where you can use statistical models to outperform your intuition. Not only can the model do the kind of reasoning we just employed faster than we can, it can do it over and over again for thousands, even millions of Marys, Susans, and Toms. In addition, it can look at hundreds of different predictive variables. The variables in the table can be combined with anything else we know about our customers—age, gender, nationality, zip code, how they redeem points in the airline's loyalty program (for trips or merchandise or some combination)—virtually simultaneously. This is what makes statistical modeling so powerful.

Let's use Susan as our example. When we dig a little deeper into what we know about her, we see that she recently changed jobs—her updated frequent-flier profile provided that information. It also showed that she moved and withdrew all her airline frequent-flier miles and used them to buy a huge flat-screen TV from one of the airline's partners. We don't know the reason for all this activity, but we do know that other female customers Susan's age (she just turned thirty-six, her profile tells us) who also did similar things stopped flying as much with the airline. (It could be as simple as a new job with less travel or wanting to start a family.) Whatever the reasons, it is safe to estimate, as the algorithm did, that the airline will be getting less revenue from her.

This frequent-flier story would help me demystify the process of statistical modeling for people. The point I would make to them is that if you create a detailed list of your customers—not only their names but other information (age, gender, profession, income, how much they have spent, etc.)—you can get a general idea of how much they will buy from you in the future by comparing them to your best customers.

Today, to get a firmer handle on those future sales, you will need to hire a statistician to do the kind of modeling that I did for the airline. But in the future—within three or four years—I expect there will be software to allow you to do this on your own. Heck, Google may even make it available for free.

The Model in Fuller Detail

The airline example focused on one of the three components that make up lifetime value: the future change (increase or decrease) of revenues from a customer. However, sometimes extracting more value out of a customer base requires a model that includes the two other variables as well—current value and length of the relationship. This would be the case for a large retail chain. For the purposes of this example, let's assume such a chain—call it Retailco.—hired us to improve the value of their customer base. We started by ranking every household's lifetime value so that Retailco. could treat each differently. (Obviously customers with the greatest potential LTV would get more than their fair attention from the company.)

Retailco. had about 1,500 stores. Their customers, as you might expect, generated enormous amounts of data. All told the company had 20 million households in their database, and for each household they know what the customer bought, as well as when, how often, and where. The size of the database is intimidating. But for data crunchers it is an absolute dream!

Retailco. had already done extensive work with relationship marketing specialists to help them get the maximum out of their existing customer base. They had implemented some of the biggest and most sophisticated loyalty programs in the retail industry. Now they wanted to put in place a lifetime value model that would enable them to target the chain's best customers (both current and potential) so that they could increase their value even further over time. The outcome of the model would be simple: We would know what every specific household was likely to spend with the stores over the next three years (a "lifetime" in the fast-moving world of retail!).

While the goal was simple, the math required was anything but. We had to begin by mapping out what LTV meant conceptually for Retailco. We came up with the approach outlined in the diagram below. What follows may be the most complicated statistical model in this book. If you make it through the next couple of paragraphs, you will not only have earned a gold star but you will have the ability to impress your friends and family by explaining the underlying principles of a Markov Chain.

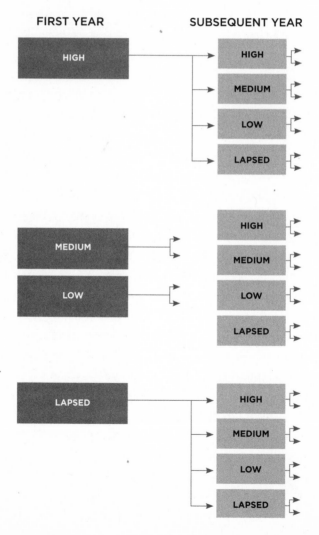

As you can see, we put the customers in four different buckets based on how much they spent. "Lapsed" meant households that hadn't made a purchase at one of the stores in twelve months.

We then defined a household's LTV as follows:

$$LTV = (\text{probability of future states}) \times (\text{future state values})$$

This means that a person's LTV is partly made up of the likelihood that she will be in one of the brackets—high, medium, low, or lapsed—in the next three years and partly by the value of a high, medium, and low household in the future. In order to calculate LTV, we would first have to predict the likelihood that someone in the high bucket was going to stay there or become medium, low, or lapsed in the next year. Then we would multiply these likelihoods with the average value of customers in those value states.

It sounds complicated but really isn't. Here is how it worked: Let's say we concluded that a high-value customer spent $1,000 a year, a medium customer spent $500, and a low one spent $50. And let's say that I am a high-value customer.

We would then build two models. The first model would predict the likelihood I would stay as a customer (using techniques I described in the airline example). And the second model would predict the likelihood I would remain a high-value customer or become a medium- or low-value one.

Let's say that these models showed I have a 20 percent chance to become a noncustomer, a 10 percent chance to become low, a 30 percent chance to become medium, and a 40 percent chance to stay at high. I would calculate my estimated value for year two as follows:

$$\text{Value year two} = 20\% \times 0 + 10\% \times \$50 + 30\% \times \$500 + 40\% \times \$1000 = \$555$$

That would give us our estimates for year two. We would repeat these exercises, based on projected year-two data, to see what would happen in year three.

We now had the ultimate prioritization mechanism for Retailco., enabling us to develop longer-term relationships with customers based on what we thought they were going to be worth over time. If Retailco. began communicating with its customers based on the LTV model, those campaigns would consistently outperform other campaigns. LTV modeling will identify your best customers and focus your efforts on them.

With this model in place, Retailco. went about evaluating every new customer it obtained, trying to figure out how much each would spend with them over the course of a lifetime. It starts with comparing the customer's initial purchases to what Retailco knows about their existing customers. But that first purchase can tell you only so much. Maybe 23 percent of all first-time customers who have work done on their cars become extremely valuable customers. But that purchase alone can't tell you if the new customer will be one of those 23 percent or fall into the less-valuable 77 percent.

But with the second purchase, you gain more information and can probably figure out more about the customer—hmm, they had car work done the first time; bought kids' clothes the second time; and then, when they signed up for the loyalty card, it showed they lived in the suburbs. In August, let's send them 20 percent off on back-to-school purchases and make sure they get the Mother's and Father's Day promotions as well.

If you know how you can talk to them, you can make a lot of money.

THINGS TO DO MONDAY MORNING

1. *Define what a valuable customer means for your company.* Is it someone who:

- spends a lot now?

- you expect to spend a lot in the future?

- has been a customer for a long time?

- might convince other customers to buy your brand?

- is not expensive to serve and therefore highly profitable?

- represents something else important to your company?

2. *Translate that definition of value into something you can measure and track* (using the tools identified in this chapter). It could be share of wallet, lifetime value, or something else that is particularly relevant to your firm.

3. *Sort your customers by how much they are worth to you.* You may want to classify them as: high value, medium value, and low value. Market to them accordingly.

CHAPTER THREE

DISCOVER: WHAT SHOULD YOU TALK TO CUSTOMERS ABOUT?

We now know who we should talk to. But what do we talk to them about? The obvious answer is: "About the stuff we want them to buy from us."

That's fine, of course—for us.

But people are not necessarily interested in how they can help us. They want to know what's in it for them.

You need to have a deep understanding of what people in your target audience want, and what they are interested in, in order to craft your message in such a way that you get the best possible response.

In this chapter, I will show you how to do just that.

Specifically, we will talk about how you can gather and analyze data to get a better understanding of your target audience's motivations. From there, we will look at how to create segments that group people depending on how similar their needs or motivations are. And we will introduce you to technologies that can help you predict what product or offer your customers would be most interested in. We will also see how all the free data that is available on social networks and elsewhere can teach you a lot about what your customers need and want. Finally, we will discuss new methods you can use to peek inside customers' brains so we can better understand how to serve them.

People need a reason to listen to your sales pitch. There has to be something in it for them, beyond whatever it is you are selling. You need to develop what I call a *value exchange*. The Amazon example we mentioned in Chapter 1 shows how this works. I am more than willing to allow them to track my purchasing history, because in return I will receive recommendations tailored to my interests.

Netflix is perhaps even better at creating this sort of value exchange. (Netflix organizes a contest every year for number crunchers, challenging them to improve on its recommendation algorithm. The winner gets one million dollars, an illustration of the importance Netflix attaches to the power of its recommendation algorithms.)

Netflix and Amazon underscore the point that analyzing customer data can provide clues to what customers value, and thereby guide you to effectively tailor your marketing to them—what we will be talking about in this chapter.

While Amazon and Netflix use sophisticated algorithms to sort through the data, those aren't always necessary. You can track what people are saying online about your products and services and then tweak and improve your positioning. For example, Caesars learned that people who stayed at their Paris hotel in Las Vegas loved the stunning views of the Las Vegas Strip they had from their rooms. As a result, Caesars changed the picture on its website to feature it. The company also discovered that people who stayed at their hotels were deeply interested in the amenities, such as room size, and details about dining options and services the hotel offered So, it began to include such information as the square footage of its suites, menus, and the like on its website. The result of the changes: Online bookings climbed by more than 10 percent. This is a simple example of why it is key to understand your customers' needs and wants: What's important to them, what they like, what they hate—in short, understanding what makes them tick in order to figure out what to talk to them about. Once you truly understand your customers, you can tailor your message, your offer, the way you talk to them, and even the channels you use to reach them (more on this later). Data can help you deliver these insights; and the impact, as the millions in increased sales at Caesars show, can be huge if you get it right.

That's why people like my colleague Mie Demin are so

valuable. Mie is a sponge who soaks in information from all sorts of sources—books, trend reports, market research, opinion leaders—and then uses everything she learned to jump easily from one topic to another in her search for consumer insights. But while it was impressive, I initially found her very hard to work with. As an analyst, I am programmed to look at large volumes of data and reduce the complexity, to summarize, as soon as possible. Agency planners such as Mie—people charged with coming up with consumer insights—are trained to expand first by relentlessly asking questions not always in a particular order to try to capture every possibility—and to sum up later. They seemed to lack any method. The information appeared chaotic and counterproductive, and often felt irritating. I just wanted Mie to get to the point, the proverbial bottom line. What had she found that we could act on? It took me a while to realize that she was going about it the right way. We couldn't know what was important until we considered everything.

You may not have "planners" at your company. But you certainly can pair people who are looking at all the sexy little numbers you have with people who take a broader, more intuitive point of view.

In our business, planners are the bridge between the strategy and the creative idea. The best one I've ever worked with is my friend Colin Mitchell, the worldwide planning director at Ogilvy. He has more information in his head than anyone I have ever met. He can think very creatively, but what sets him apart as a planner is his ability to rationally simplify the complex. I have been in many meetings where a room full of people would argue about what the right strategy should be. Colin would come in, listen for ten minutes, and then summarize the entire conversation in one sentence, afterward laying out, in a couple of simple, clear bullet points, how the strategy should unfold.

Colin and I used to write a blog together called thedouble think, http://thedoublethink.com. The name comes from George Orwell's term for the ability to hold two conflicting ideas in your head and reconcile them. We divided the blog into two parts. On the left side of the screen, I wrote about math and analytics. On the right side, Colin commented about just about everything else. The juxtaposition of the approaches—sometimes we wrote about similar topics, most times we didn't—is something that people told us they found "intriguing" and "stimulating."

The upshot after reading our blog: You see the results of the left and right brains combined. It is very much a model for how today, in this world where tons of data are being generated, the combination of analytics and planning can come up with very powerful insights.

To illustrate, let's take a look at one of the most often used information sources for driving consumer insights—market research.

In qualitative market research, the researcher will talk to only a handful of consumers (often, ten to twenty), either individually or in a group. Because the researcher talks to only a few people, he can go into a lot of detail about why consumers are purchasing certain brands, what their needs are, and what the real underlying motives are for making purchasing decisions. You might have participated in one of these interviews yourself. They can last a couple of hours. One variation of this approach is the research focus group. A number of consumers in a room have a group discussion about a category, a brand, or even a campaign idea.

You can also segment by motivation or attitudes to find groups of consumers who feel a certain way and have the same needs. In a way, you are trying to find archetypes of consumers. As we said before, an archetype is a prototype such as a NASCAR Dad or (back in the day) a Yuppie.

Different types of personalities will interact with products and brands differently, so it is important for you to understand these different personalities in order to reach them effectively. It may sound very Jungian, but it is a fact that people make purchasing decisions for psychological reasons as well as rational reasons. The degree to which behavior is driven by rationality, as opposed to emotion, is subject to a lot of discussion. But as a quantitative analyst—the archetype, perhaps, for rationality—I can tell you that I firmly believe that in most categories there is much less rationality involved in purchasing decisions than you might think.

Take me, for example. Convinced we needed a new TV for our apartment, I spent hours online reading everything available so I could get the perfect one. My research convinced me that a 42-inch Panasonic plasma television was exactly what we needed. But when I went to the store, the 52-inch Sony LCD presented such large and vivid images, I bought that instead.

Qualitative research can provide insightful information, but the small sample size requires validation to determine whether what people told you is true for a large group of people or only for them. Quantitative research uses shorter surveys with a much larger group that could easily climb into the thousands. But the more people involved, the more data you have, and the happier we data analytics folks feel. Data is our raw material and the more raw material we have, the easier it is to find key insights, spot trends, and confirm the various models we build.

By combining the results of quantitative and qualitative research, you can produce results you are confident about. Steve Naert, best man at my wedding and a friend of mine since we were both seven, works for Censydiam, an Antwerp-based research firm that digs into the psyches of people. Steve's company believes that "it is easy to observe and measure the overt rationales consumers use to justify purchases. As with an

iceberg, however, the most powerful drivers of consumer satis-
faction strategies lie beneath the surface. And that is where his
firm concentrates its research. "Below the waterline, we find
the feelings and emotions, the motivations, urges and needs
we cannot see."

Censydiam not only has psychologists, but also a quant department where analysts like me trawl through data from quantitative research and trends to come up with consumer insights.
One of the most inventive pieces of analysis I have ever seen
came from collaboration between Censydiam and Helmut Gaus,
a professor at the University of Ghent in Belgium. We who work
with sexy little numbers are always looking for ways to predict, based on the data, what our customers and prospects might
do. Censydiam and Gaus were no different. But they started by
asking an intriguing—if offbeat—question: Are changes in the
economy caused by changes in the mental state of society?

It is tempting to dismiss the correlations between rising
hemlines and higher stock prices as just a coincidence. But
Gaus takes the question of the relation between the economy
and social behavior seriously.

Gaus's theory starts with the work of Russian statistician
Nikolaj Kondratieff, who in 1925 discovered long macroeconomic waves that would repeat themselves every fifty years
throughout history, through alternating periods of growth
and decline.

Kondratieff paid a heavy price for this discovery. His predictions that the economy would eventually decline were not
popular with Stalin, who sent him to Siberia to be executed.

Much has been written about whether the Kondratieff
waves actually exist. Not everyone is convinced, but the truth
is, they have remained reasonably predictive to this day.

Gaus was most interested in the causes of the waves.
Most people thought they were driven by macroeconomic

forces—GDP, the unemployment rate, and the like. Gaus was convinced that the real drivers were psychological. He argued that the Kondratieff waves coincided and in some cases even followed what he called *anxiety waves*, which are predictive of changes in tastes, values, and behavior.

To prove his point, Gaus gathered data on women's fashion trends. He found that in periods of high anxiety, women wear less color, fewer patterns, higher necklines, and longer skirts. In periods of lower anxiety, they wear brighter colors and patterns, lower necklines, and short skirts. This allowed him to create an anxiety wave based on the prevalence of these fashion trends over time.

He found startling correlations between anxiety levels and all sorts of indicators such as marriages, births, employment levels, suicides, and investment levels over time.

The idea that fluctuations in the economy are caused by the collective levels of anxiety is interesting but hard to prove. Data on the mental state of society is scarce, which is why Gaus used data on fashion as a proxy. There is, however, a relatively new information source that holds extremely rich information on what's on people's minds—it's the data held by search engines. Knowing what people search for, and how that changes over time, could potentially lead to a barometer of society's mental state.

Now, Gaus's theory has yet to be definitively proven. But I love the idea of combining real hard data with deep consumer insights to come up with ideas that could provide useful information. So I studied the Censydiam approach thoroughly (less by studying their research papers and more by having conversations with Steve over a few beers in our favorite Antwerp pubs). It was important information to have. For example, the previous chapter discussed how we used data to figure out which BT customers to talk to. But we wanted to do more than just find the right people. We needed to develop compelling communications that would help grow BT's business. So we really needed to get underneath the skin of the British small and medium businesses so we could figure out what we should talk to them about.

BRITISH TELECOM FROM SOFT TO HARD

In order to truly understand the BT customers, we now needed to understand both sides of their brains. We had hard, data-driven segmentation information about those customers, as discussed in the previous chapter, but now we required a needs-based segmentation study. We worked with our planners and the Henley Centre (now called the Futures Company), a specialist trend-watching company based in the UK, to try and really understand BT's business-to-business customers. The idea was to come up with something insightful *and* at the same time linked to the data we had, so we could not only craft a message that appealed to small and medium businesses, but also identify which ones would be most interested in which type of message.

We took a three-step approach:

First, we created an exhaustive list of needs BT could potentially fulfill for small businesses.

Next, we would have to identify which of those needs were most important to the small and medium-sized business customers.

Finally, we would have to discover whether there were different types of small businesses for which these needs might be different. For example, does a service company with five million dollars in revenues have the same communication needs as a five-million-dollar manufacturing company?

We started by creating a list of every possible need we could think of and came up with a list of seventeen.

NEW CHANNELS & MARKETS
- Entering new geographical markets
- Developing new distribution channels
- Getting new products or services to market

CUSTOMER FOCUS
- Growing your customer base
- Improving customer service & relationships
- Increasing revenue from your existing customers

OPERATIONAL EFFICIENCY
- Improving the management of your supply and stock chain
- Improving the management of purchasing and procurement
- Improving the management of your internal processes
- Ensuring continuity of critical business systems and processes

BUSINESS ADMINISTRATION
- Reducing the effort spent on administering government rules and regulations
- Improving management of company or financial accounts
- Improving the management of information technology

WORKFORCE EFFICIENCY
- Sharing information with colleagues
- Enabling employees to work more flexibly (job sharing or working from home)
- Enabling employees to work on the move

SECURITY
- Ensuring the business is protected against crime & other risks, such as on-line fraud, computer viruses or burglary

Since it was impossible to concentrate on all seventeen items, our second task was defining which ones were most important to our target. We did so through both quantitative research, which means we interviewed a big sample of small businesses and asked them which needs were most important. To make it clear, we presented what we discovered in a pie chart.

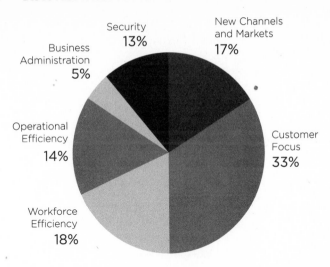

Finally, we wanted to create different segments based on which needs customers found to be important. The statistical technique—one I love—used for this is *cluster analysis*. You let the data speak and form different groups of customers. But then you need to make a judgment call on whether these groups make sense and are actionable. The combination of data and interpretation always makes this a fun exercise because it is half science, half art.

Let's say we interviewed people at a thousand small and medium businesses and asked them about only one need: the importance, on a scale of 1 to 10, of managing their supply chain. Let's say that the responses (represented by dots in the illustration below) looked like this:

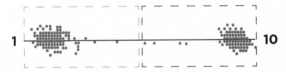

Supply chain management is not at all important

Supply chain management is very important

In this case it is clear that there are two camps: companies that find supply chain management (SCM) important and companies that don't. The cluster analysis would be pretty simple here. We could draw boxes as boundaries around the two clusters that clearly seem to exist.

Now let's assume that we asked two independent questions about the importance of managing their supply chain and enabling employees to work on the move. And let's assume the results of the answers to these two questions looked like the illustration below.

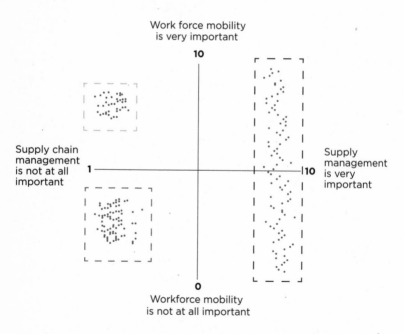

As you can see, we found that the three segments are: people who find SCM important (right), those who find SCM not important but who find mobility important (top left), and people who find neither SCM nor mobility important (bottom left).

Now it was very easy to draw these boxes visually. But trying to explain to a computer how to do it is harder! One way is by telling the computer to use the concept of distance to draw the best boundaries. Here is how a cluster analysis briefs a computer. We tell it to:

- *Minimize the distances between the dots that belong to the same group.* This ensures that the people within each group are very similar.

- *Maximize the distances between the centers of the different groups* (to replicate the drawing you see on page 74). You do that because you want the groups themselves to be visually distinct so they are easier to find.

If it were just a matter of asking about two or three needs, we wouldn't need the computer at all. We could see and draw the dots ourselves and put the borders around the clusters. But, remember, we didn't ask about two needs, but seventeen. That is beyond our abilities. (Don't believe me? Just try doing half as many; you will go nuts.)

When we had the computer sort all seventeen needs—and I will spare you all the dots and the boxes—we found that there were five main clusters. These five groups were all very different when it came to how much importance they attached to the seventeen needs, but the SMBs within a segment were all very similar when it came to deciding which of the seventeen needs they found important. (Again, in the list on page 76, ICT stands for integrated communications technology, the catchall term BT used for advanced communications offerings.)

The payoff from this was huge. Dividing the market up this way gave BT an opportunity to talk to each group differently. For segment two, those who are all about focusing on their

- SEGMENT 1 - BASIC NEEDS (16%):
  Small "lifestyle" businesses whose main focus is to provide regular employment & income for their owners. Low level of needs for ICT.

- SEGMENT 2 - CUSTOMER FOCUS (33%):
  Customer-facing service companies driven by a decrease to build stronger customer relationships & improve service. Needs relate to customer focus—based technology.

- SEGMENT 3 - OPERATIONAL EFFICIENCY (14%):
  Midsized businesses driven by need to streamline their production processes and improve customer service. High need of technologies that improve operational process.

- SEGMENT 4 - FLEXIBLE & SECURE (18%):
  Optimistic, technology-reliant service industries for whom business agility is a priority. ICT savvy with very high needs for technologies benefiting flexibility and security.

- SEGMENT 5 - HIGH NEEDS (19%):
  Young, technologically savvy businesses whose primary motivation is to grow & expand. High needs for all dimensions.

customers, we would talk about security in a completely different way than we would to segment three, whose members are concerned about internal operations. For the former, the conversation might be about how BT's technology could provide security for a client's customers; for the latter, we would stress the benefits of BT's solutions for the security of internal systems.

This needs-based segmentation gave us a powerful tool to tailor our communications.

THIS APPROACH CAN COMPLEMENT WHAT YOU ARE ALREADY DOING

You can combine the needs-based approach with whatever segmenting work you are already doing to gain additional insights about your customers. That's what we did at Cisco. As you will recall from Chapter 1, we did a segment analysis based on how much a customer spent in the category (technology) and how much of that spending they did with Cisco. While the sales force eagerly adopted our Value Spectrum framework, some folks in the marketing department were less enthusiastic at first, because they already had their own segmentation approach. The marketing department segmentation put customers in four tiers based on their attitudes toward technology (advice driven, price driven, cutting edge, and enterprise-like, i.e., acting like a Fortune 100 company). While some of the marketers saw these two segmentation frameworks as competing, it was clear to me that they were very complementary. The Value Spectrum told Cisco who to talk to, and the attitude-based segmentation they already had in place told them what to talk about.

I tried to show how the two approaches could work together through the following diagram:

	ADVICE DRIVEN	PRICE DRIVEN	CUTTING EDGE	ENTERPRISE - LIKE
	◯	◯	◯	◯
	◯	◯	◯	◯
	◯	◯	◯	◯
	◯	◯	◯	◯

In the rows reading left to right, you can find the Value Spectrum segments; and from the top down, you see the attitudinal segments. The size of the bubbles indicates how many companies fit in each cell. The bigger the bubble, the more customers there are in the segment.

Look at the first row across, which represents the Nuggets, Cisco's best customers. There are more cutting-edge nuggets than any other type. However, there are still a lot of nuggets that are advice driven, price driven and enterprise-like. Using both segmentations at the same time not only allows you to find the nuggets, it allows you to tailor your messaging to the needs of each one.

Initially for Cisco we found sixteen segments—too many to create different strategies and communications for. So we ended up grouping them in three segments (based on what made sense intuitively and based on how we could treat them differently).

- *Romance:* These were the most valuable and high-potential customers (Nuggets and Jackpots), for whom the Cisco brand fit was the best (i.e., Nuggets and Jackpots who also appeared in the cutting edge and enterprise-like segments of the chart on page 79). We needed to romance them to make sure we kept them.

- *Defense:* These were high-value customers (Nuggets) for whom the Cisco brand wasn't perfect (they fell into the advice-driven and price-driven squares). We needed to make sure we kept these important customers who might be open to courting from our competitors.

- *Vanilla:* These were all the other customers for whom we decided initially not to differentiate our communications.

	ADVICE DRIVEN	PRICE DRIVEN	CUTTING EDGE	ENTERPRISE - LIKE
	2. DEFENSE			1. ROMANCE
			3. VANILLA	

By focusing on only these three segments we were able very quickly to implement tailored and segmented marketing efforts. Cluster analysis can be done not only quickly but also very cheaply. For example, just two weeks before the agency was going to pitch the account, I got a call asking if we could run this sort of segmentation for IKEA.

After initially saying it was impossible—and who wouldn't, since there simply wasn't enough time—my team got it done. We couldn't survey a huge number of IKEA's customers, but we could (and did) talk to a representative sample. We found three distinct categories when it came to the purchasing of home furnishings and five when it came to do-it-yourselfers, categories the competition was not paying sufficient attention to. The cost of the survey: just $3,000, since we asked all the research questions online. And, oh yes, we won the account.

AUTOMATED RECOMMENDATION TOOLS

There are other techniques, in addition to the attitudinal segmentations we just talked about, that can help tailor your communications. For example, market basket analysis—literally finding out what is in the customer's shopping cart—can often reveal all you need to know simply because it tells a great deal about the products he is interested in. It became popular with retailers in the '90s because of the "beer and diapers story."

According to the tale, a never-named US retailer used statistical modeling to analyze all its shopping baskets—what their customers bought during each shopping trip. They noticed that on Friday nights beer was often in the same shopping cart as diapers. When they dug a little deeper they found that women were sending their husbands to the store on a Friday night to pick up some diapers for junior. As long as they were there, the guys would pick up a six-pack on the way out. The supermarket used this insight to move the beer next to the diapers and they significantly increased their beer and diaper sales as a result.

Great anecdote; unfortunately, it turns out it was made up by a consultant trying to sell the value of market basket analysis. No retailer ever made such a finding. But though fictional, the story explains perfectly why market basket analysis can be a very powerful tool. Let's use another fictional anecdote to dive deeper.

A large direct-mail merchant was considering product-specific communications and needed advice on improving its targeting. They wanted an insight into product usage (specifically which products were bought together and which were not). And they wanted to use these insights for better targeting of product specific communications.

This merchant has 3,360 different products in their database. To help them out, our first step would be to group like things together. For simplicity's sake, we will use a two-level classification. The first level lumps those products into 20 product families; the second level lumps them into 159 smaller families. In each instance, we would analyze every single product that could be bought with every single other one. As you intuitively understand, the number of combinations to be analyzed grows exponentially with the number of product families.

After completing that analysis, our next task would be building a model that would predict the likelihood of different products being bought together (within the same transaction or within a certain time frame). The model needs to be tested by sending the same marketing communication—let's posit a commemorative Kennedy half-dollar—to two groups of customers. The first group would be selected from the database using the market basket analysis rules (we wanted people who had bought other commemorative coin reissues). The second group would be selected randomly without using the rules. Here's what the formula for that market basket analysis looked like:

$$A = B \text{ \& } C \text{ \& } D \rightarrow N, P, S$$

On the surface it seems like gibberish without context. But it is really straightforward.

- *A = the product* (product or product family) for which the rule predicts a sale. What I am trying to predict in this case is whether you are going to buy commemorative half-dollars when are shopping on the merchant's website. The A in this case would stand for the half-dollar.

- *B, C, and D = the predictors* (used to predict the purchase of A). These are the other products you might be buying (other commemorative coins, authentic memorabilia, historically themed knicknacks) that could indicate your likelihood to also have Kennedy half-dollars in your basket.

- *N = coverage in absolute numbers* (the total number of customers who have bought products B, C and D in the same transaction).

- P = *the probability someone will buy A*, given he has already bought B, C and D.

- S = *support* (percent of total population who have bought B, C, D, and A).

To test this model we would send the same marketing communication—in this case, a direct mail piece—to two groups of customers. The first group would be selected from the database using the market basket analysis rules. The second would be selected randomly without using the rules. Success would mean that the conversion rate for the first group was considerably higher—perhaps as much as five times—than that for the second group.

If You Like This, You Love That

Automated recommendation tools such as market basket analysis have become very popular in the online environment. As we said, Amazon's and Netflix's recommendation engines are probably the best known. They make product suggestions—if you liked that book or movie, you are likely to like this one—by comparing you to people who have read similar books (or seen similar movies). It gives real value to the consumer. I love how Netflix recommends movies to me I have never heard of. It's one of the main reasons I am prepared to pay their subscription fee, and Netflix understands that. They track how many (and what percentage) of movies I rent, based on their suggestions. What Amazon and Netflix are doing is just what the supermarkets do when they try to predict if you are going to buy apples and bananas during your same visit to the store, or when the postal service we talked about tries to figure which products to offer in combination to reach their stamp collectors.

Off-the-shelf solutions are now available that can help personalize your marketing communications much as Amazon and Netflix provide. These tools enable smaller companies to level the playing field and compete with industry giants. Those who do this type of research about customers and then specifically tailor their recommendations for those customers have a huge competitive advantage. As noted, most of the off-the-shelf solutions for what we have been discussing are readily available, not ridiculously expensive for the insights they reveal, and they work really well. There should be no excuse for you not to use them. You should check out companies like Audience Science, Proclivity, and Netmining, to name just a few. I especially like Netmining, and that's not just because the founder, Toon Van Parys, is a fellow Belgian.

Netmining gathers data from consumers via real-time web browsing. The data is used to predict what a customer will be interested in buying, and Netmining automatically serves up advertising content in line with a person's interests. (If you wonder how advertisers can follow you around online—you go to CNN.com and see a specific ad for blue jeans; you go to fashionista.com, and there it is again—you will find out in Chapter 4, "How Do You Find Them?")

Tools like these can bring amazing results that demonstrate the power of offering the right product to the right person. For example, once it started using this tool, Fiat saw a 350 percent increase in lead volume and a 500 percent increase in sales conversion.

The really cool thing about Netmining is the visualization of results. It enabled the people at Fiat to easily see which vehicles people are most interested in and how likely it is they will purchase the car. You can check out a live demo of this visualization on their site.

So far in this chapter, we have discussed how to understand our customers or prospects better through analyzing the data we get from research (qualitative or quantitative), from transactional data, such as the sources we described in Chapter 2 on who to talk to, and from web behavior data. These data sources have been around for quite some time. Now let's turn our attention to intriguing data sources that have become available fairly recently.

Text Data Derived from What People Write

People type a lot these days. They participate in forums, write status updates on social networks, and make comments on blogs; a lot of them even have their own blogs. If you think about it, all that text is data. And, even better, it's free. The challenge isn't capturing it. All you need is a simple scraping tool, which is exactly like what it sounds like. It "reads" the sites you are interested in monitoring and copies (or scrapes) what you have told it into a database. Capturing this information might be easy, but analysis is a lot harder. Earlier, I gave you a couple of examples about how we can teach computers to look at data in a certain way. This is relatively easy when you want them to look at numbers. It's a lot harder when you want them to look at text. But it is not impossible.

There are software packages available that can analyze large volumes of text and give you an idea of the topics people are talking about, how many people are talking about these topics, and even how people are feeling about them. Here is an example that text-mining company Visible Technologies gave me a couple of years ago:

> I hate the way George W. Bush is constantly being bashed. So he makes stupid mistakes in his grammar—big deal! His immigration policies are right on! We have to be willing to take a hard stand. I think he's crazy with the privatization of social security, though.

I'm not sure if the troops in Iraq would vote for him again, but they're doing what has to be done.

Bobstud189

Early (read: primitive) text-mining software would have counted the number of positive versus negative words it recognized and would have concluded the sentiment of the post was negative.

SENTIMENT		TOPIC
Positive	on	George W Bush
Positive	on	Immigration Policies
Negative	on	Social Security
Neutral	on	War in Iraq
Positive	on	Overall

The problem is, while the technology would have classified the words correctly, it would have come to the wrong conclusion. The comment about the former president was at least somewhat positive.

Newer technologies would actually be able to parse out that comment into subcomments and determine their sentiment. A lot more information would thereby be extracted from the blog post. We can see modern algorithms allow computers more accurately to register and categorize the topics and sentiment of what people are talking about online.

There are still plenty of challenges with this tool. I was recently talking to the brand manager for Axe deodorant. He said that when they first implemented it they saw what appeared to be a spike in interest in the product at the start of the recession. Were people talking more about their deodorant when times are tough? Not exactly. People were talking about how they were worried about getting axed or other people getting axed, as in *fired*. It seems that computers still find it hard to see the difference between a conversation about body hygiene and a life-altering event such as losing your job.

Nevertheless, companies have started to use these social media analytic tools successfully to listen to what is going on in the blogosphere. You can use this technology to analyze how people are talking about your brand. But you might want to start with just reading the comments people write.

That's what we did in the Caesars example I mentioned earlier. Caesars periodically takes the fifty most recent five-star (highest rating) reviews of the hotels it owns from the popular travel review site TripAdvisor and examines them for insights. They organize the comments by theme—physical hotel attributes, location, hotel amenities, casino comments, service—and then further search out what the people said they really liked—what caused them to give the hotel the five-star review. Sometimes, as in the case of the reviews of its Paris hotel, the results are surprising. As I mentioned before, what people love about the Paris is the view of Las Vegas Boulevard ("The Strip") they can see from their rooms. As a result of this insight, today when you go to the Paris hotel landing page (ParisLasVegas.com) you now see a picture of the view you'll have from the hotel, as well as the hotel itself. Bookings are up as a result.

Whenever I discuss Caesars, someone asks what text-mining software or algorithm we used to discover the insight. It always amuses me to see their reaction when I tell them we just read comments that were posted on TripAdvisor.com.

Something similar happened at IBM. In studying what its customers were saying online, the company noticed that very few people were mentioning how wonderful its technology was—even though it was wonderful. Instead they talked about all the cool things the technology was letting them do. Most people don't care about how technology works—they really have no interest in understanding why it is possible to speak cell phone to cell phone; they just want to use their cell phone to reach someone else's. As a result of this insight, the focus of IBM's marketing shifted from talking about Voice over Internet Protocol (VoIP) and cloud delivery models to new and better ways to have conversations and meetings. A Lotus ad was typical. The tag line: "Lotus knows you're trying to reach the person, not their phone."

Why Feelings Are So Important

An entire new industry is springing up around how emotion influences what we decide to buy. Innerscope, a research firm that specializes in this new field, has learned that the old ways we think about advertising are inaccurate, if not completely wrong.

We have always thought that people receive a stimulus, such as an ad, think about it, and then decide on how (if at all) that ad will affect their behavior. What Innerscope has discovered is that's not at all how it works. People receive stimuli that may or may not pass the emotional filter we all have deep inside our brains. Only if the stimulus triggers an emotional response is it even considered by the rational parts of our brains. Then there is a complex interplay between rationality and emotions that determines what we do next.

The key takeaway: "Feeling" generally precedes "thinking" and "doing." This is why Innerscope has developed a set of diagnostics to measure how emotionally engaging media stimuli are. The diagnostics measure four physical changes people experience when emotionally engaged:

- *Skin conductance:* changes in sweat levels of the palms

- *Respiration:* changes in our breathing patterns

- *Heart response:* changes in our heart rate (does it literally beat faster?)

- *Movement:* changes in physical movement (does the stimulus literally cause action?)

Innerscope measures all this through a specially designed vest their respondents wear during research. The vest has built-in sensors that track these variables while a person is watching TV, browsing the web, or even walking through a store. This gives Innerscope data points on the unfiltered emotions a person experiences when exposed to communications.

Not surprisingly, they found that emotional engagement plays an important role in the effectiveness of in-store experiences, online buzz, print ads, websites, and packaging.

Innerscope complements the biometric diagnostics with advanced eye tracking that provides data on how well people receive media stimuli, as well as with more traditional research techniques that measure their rational responses.

All this raises an important question. If rationality has only a minor impact on behavior change, why are we spending so much time asking consumers what they thought of our communications and how that affected their behavior? We should probably focus more of our energy on getting a better understanding of the emotional engagement our communications created.

VoicePrism, another company specializing in understanding people's emotions, takes a slightly creepy approach. Its technology analyzes sound waves generated by the human voice. They have someone talk for ten minutes, in order to establish a baseline, and then they have the individual discuss various stimuli—advertising, in our case—that he is shown. They compare the person's reaction to the baseline to show emotions such as excitement, stress, delight, anger. The voice could be an additional data point that can give us clues about what is happening in the subconscious. I haven't seen another technology that has the potential to capture data from the subconscious for potentially thousands of consumers.

Understanding emotional responses is crucial in marketing. A famous study by the Institute of Practitioners in Advertising demonstrated that emotional advertising campaigns consistently outperform rational campaigns in terms of driving sales, share, price elasticity, loyalty, and penetration. A great example of this is the ad known as the "Cadbury's gorilla," which has been viewed about six million times on YouTube since the commercial debuted in 2007.

THINGS TO DO MONDAY MORNING

1. *Ask your customers why they buy from you.* It's best to do this through talking to a handful of representative customers and spending a lot of time with them. Their answers will very quickly give you a list of potential needs you are fulfilling. To round out that list, look online to see what people are actually saying about your brand on social networks and forums. (If you want to do it like the pros, you can hire a research agency to help facilitate these conversations. You can even use neuroscientists to find out what is in people's heads with regard to your company. Both are good ideas, but far from mandatory.)

2. *Once you have a list of potential needs,* determine which ones are most important to your customers. That can be done through quantitative research, which does not have to break the bank these days. There are plenty of online research providers who can do it fast and cheaply. Through this exercise you can also identify groups (clusters) of customers who are looking for different things from your products and services. This will allow you to create messages tailored just for them.

3. *Once you know what your customers want,* develop your products or services with that in mind. In fact, everything you do—from your website to the way you communicate with your customers—should reflect the fact that you understood what they told you.

CHAPTER FOUR

LOCATE: HOW DO YOU FIND THEM?

Now that we know whom we want to talk to and what we can talk to them about, we need to discover where these customers and prospects are so that we can hold a conversation. That's harder than you might think. Even if they don't physically move, customers are constantly looking at new media (different websites, for example) and visiting other stores. They are more like cats than dogs. They are not predictable and they cannot be trained.

The traditional way of finding prospects was twofold. One was identifying the media—TV, radio, newspapers, magazines, Internet— that the people you want to reach, watch, listen to, read, or use. The second was targeting them by geography. Most upper-middle-class people, to take one segment, live in a finite number of places.

More recently, though, we've been given a number of tools that allow us to find individuals rather than groups. The more specific and tailored the message, the greater your chances of success.

Here we will explain how you can find individuals: in databases you can build on websites yourself; through search engines; in external databases you can purchase; on advertising networks; and on social networks. These are all places where people leave behind traces of data when they visit. These data traces can be used to more accurately find the exact people you want to talk to.

Remember the Boots cucumber wipes I mentioned in Chapter 1? My wife thinks they are fantastic and is convinced they can only be found in the United Kingdom. That is not true. But they are extremely hard to find elsewhere, and that's why a lot of British expats (like my wife) buy them by the sack whenever they spot them while traveling overseas.

Let's assume Boots has noticed that sales are extraordinarily high in stores located within international airports, and its chief marketing officer (CMO) has asked us to develop a marketing campaign that targets expats. How would we find our targets?

Well,

- We could try and get to know what newspapers or magazines expats read and run an ad there.

- We could try and find these expats geographically and target them accordingly. We could even do a wet-wipe mailing to zip codes where we know a lot of British expats live.

- We know that expats visiting home will pass through UK airports at some point, so we could buy advertising billboards in the terminals. We also know a lot of them will continue their travels by train, and some will rent cars. We could advertise in train stations located near international airports and near the rental car counters.

- We could also try and find the addresses of the expats abroad.

- We could beef up our presence in places where we know British expats convene—for example, Nevada Smiths in New York City (slogan: "Where football is religion"—only in America is football called soccer), a pub that shows all English Premier League soccer games. Every Saturday morning the pub is jammed with British expats. We could hang posters there that remind the mostly male crowd to bring the world's best wet wipes home to their lady.

Boots could also start to build up an internal database of expats hooked on its wet wipes. Customers enrolled in the expat program could get free shipping. In exchange, the company could ask them a few questions to gather valuable data for Boots (e.g., how much do you consume, how often do you come back to the United Kingdom, and do you have any friends who would like to join the expat program?). This would allow Boots to build a database of expats to communicate with on a regular basis. And we could probably buy external lists of addresses of British expats as well. This could help us build up that database even faster.

What else? Well, when someone googles British pubs in New York City, we can assume a higher probability they are British expats. We could buy search impressions for our wet wipes for terms British expats would look for ("British Pubs," "British Restaurants," "Manchester United Soccer," and the like). We could do the same with online advertising: We could target visitors to the BBC website from the United States with Boots wet wipes ads. And we could get even more specific. Later we will describe how we can see if someone looked for flights to the United Kingdom online, how we can then follow them around the web and serve up a Boots wet-wipes banner ad when they visit pages *elsewhere.* We could also find British expats easily on Facebook and other social networks. We could invite them to join the Boots cucumber wet wipe fan page on Facebook.

The possibilities seem endless. But we can start our search for potential customers through four main actions:

- *Media planning:* Gain a thorough understanding of the profiles of consumers of certain media and match those profiles to the profile of your target audience.

- *Geographic targeting:* Understand where your targets live.

- *Individual targeting:* Exactly what it sounds like: Learn how to reach a specific person via her physical address, email address, or online cookie.

- *Panels:* A panel is a representative group of a market segment you want to target, such as ex-pats. You can ask them questions and get to know your target audience. While panels are usually used as a research tool, some very big panels are targetable in and of themselves. This means you can actually send them tailored messages based on what you know about them.

Let's take all these options one at a time.

Media planning. Media planning is the way most companies have targeted their potential customers. It's straightforward. You buy the media you think your target will be reading or watching. This is done—using very basic math—through matching the profiles of your target audience with the various media available.

So where do we get the data on who reads or watches which media? Most countries have cross-category surveys that provide media planners the majority of data they need. For example, the Target Group Index (TGI) panel in the United Kingdom and Mediamark Research & Intelligence (MRI) in the United States run big surveys asking people about websites they visit, TV shows they watch, magazines they read, etc. They also ask them about which brands they buy and what their sociodemographic profile is (age, gender, where they live, etc.).

Here is an example of an analysis we did for a company that provides video on demand (VOD) over the Internet. The company had identified its target as any household that has broadband Internet access at home, any Visa credit card, and owns a DVR (a broad audience indeed). We first found out from TGI and MRI which broad-based media this target audience consumed, so we could begin thinking about where we wanted to place our ads. (In the table that follows OOH stands for out-of-home advertising.)

HAS HOME BROADBAND & ANY VISA CREDIT CARD & DVR

QUINTILE	TV	Radio	Magazines	Newspapers	OOH	Online	
I	67	87	137	118	132	195	highest
II	103	114	118	97	124	157	
III	116	128	111	107	110	105	
IV	120	105	85	101	83	30	
V	94	67	50	76	51	13	lowest

At the top of the table you can see the different media we wanted to analyze. On the left-hand side are five quintiles, five groups of equal size, ranked from high to low in terms of how much time individuals in that group spend in each medium. Here is how to interpret the table. Let's take the number 195 at the top right of the table. It shows that the index for our target audience in Quintile 1 for online is 195. What does that mean? It means that if you compare our target audience (households that have broadband Internet access at home, have a credit card, and have a DVR) to the US national average, you see almost twice the number of people spending a lot of time online. The national average index is 100; so our index of 195 is almost double. In other words, if we were to advertise online, we would find almost twice the number of people in our target audience among the heavy online users compared to the national average. This shows that online is probably a good place to find our target audience.

The opposite is true for TV. Of the heavy TV viewers (quintile 1 in the TV column), we find a much smaller proportion of our target audience (67 compared to 100 for the national average). So this quick table shows us that online, OOH (out-of-home; think: billboards), and magazines are the best places to find our target audience.

The next question we need to answer is where online are

these folks spending their time—which sites are they visiting? We would use the exact same approach. But this time we are going to get much more granular. Rather than comparing online vs. TV vs. radio vs. . . . whatever, we compare site A vs. site B vs. site C. And we would do the same for specific magazines, etc.

The following table from the research we did for the video-on-demand client shows the websites that had higher than average indices. (If TV had popped, we could have done the same for specific TV shows.) This is where this specific target audience is spending a disproportionate amount of time. This is where they can be found.

HIGHEST	ABOVE AVERAGE
Tripadvisor.com	Wikipedia.org
CNET.com	Shopzilla.com
CBS.Sportsline.com	Yahoo! Sports
WSJ.com	NFL.com
Superpages.com	Orbitz.com
Bizrate.com	WebMD.com
IMDb.com	Ticketmaster.com
iVillage.com	FOXNews.com
Bankrate.com	Fox.com
ZDNet.com	YellowPages.com
MLB.com	ABC.com
Gmail	WhitePages.com
(Index Range from 200 to 285)	MSNBC.com
Priceline.com	Yahoo! Movies
Maps.google.com (Google Maps)	NBC.com
Overstock.com	Weather.com
Amazon.com	Ebay.com
Expedia.com	MSN Maps & Directions (Live
Travelocity.com	Search Maps)
About.com	CNN.com
ESPN.com	Hotels.com
Moviefone.com	NYTimes.com
USAToday.com	Other Internet Activities
CBS.com	Disney.com
FoxSports.com	NASCAR.com

No matter what medium you use, the principles are the same. Here's what you need to do:

1. Find the profile of the people you would like to target.

2. Then find media properties with a high proportion of those readers, viewers, listeners, or visitors.

3. Contact those media properties and buy space or time.

Let's say, for example, that American Express knows that a lot of its target users—both existing customers to whom they want to present an offer so they will increase their spending and also people they would like to become customers—are affluent and live in the northeastern United States. American Express can then use the techniques we described to find websites where affluent households from the Northeast frequently visit. This will give the company a short list of sites where they should buy media space.

Assume CNNMoney is one of those sites. American Express can buy, for example, 10,000 impressions—meaning, their ad will appear 10,000 times on the screen for a certain period of time. (Later in this chapter we will see how advanced technology has made it possible to make this process much more precise so that American Express can make sure that only people they want to target can see those ads.)

Geographic targeting. You can also find your targets geographically. To use our Boots wet wipes example, I know there are probably more British expats in New York City than there are in Dallas. Not just in absolute numbers but also in relative terms, as a percentage of the population. It is therefore probably better to target New York than Dallas. But even within New York City, I can further refine my targeting. I don't have the data, although I could easily get it, but I think there are more British expats in the East Village of Manhattan than in the borough of Staten Island. And, of course, in the United

States, we can actually target based on zip code. Every zip code has a number of statistics that have been derived from a number of sources that give you sociodemographic data that can be used in your marketing, so we can refine our research of the East Village further. (It turns out there are three different zip codes in the East Village.)

These zip codes also can be rolled up to designated market areas (DMAs). Nielsen Media Research, which coined the term, uses it to identify TV stations that best reach a specific area of the country. So, to continue using our NYC example, the New York DMA would include some viewers in New Jersey and Connecticut as well. Surveys such as MRI can perform analysis for different DMAs, allowing you to pick the ones you would like to target.

Here is how we did this for the online video provider mentioned earlier. The figure below shows the largest 81 DMAs (there are 210 nationwide) for our target of households that have broadband Internet access at home, a credit card, and a DVR.

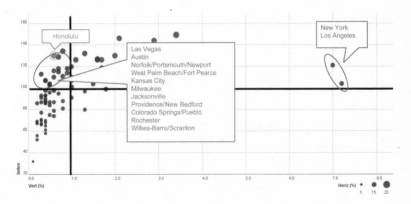

The DMAs are mapped along two axes. The vertical shows an index very similar to the ones we described above. But rather than calculate it for different media, we calculated it for DMAs. The higher the index, the higher the proportion of our target audience that lives within the DMA. If the index is higher than 100, it means that there are more households of our target audience's profile in that DMA than on average nationally. You therefore want to go after the DMAs above the black line in the middle of the graph.

The horizontal axis shows what proportion of all households that have broadband Internet access at home, a credit card, and a DVR live in that particular DMA. You can clearly see the New York and Los Angeles DMAs on the far right of the graph. That just makes sense. They are the two biggest DMAs. This client asked us to identify smaller DMAs that have a very high proportion of the target audience, so we can target them most efficiently. Those are the ones at the top left of the graph (Las Vegas, Austin, Kansas City, etc.).

We can even go more granular. One of the smaller DMAs that were identified as having a high proportion of the target audience in this exercise was Honolulu. When we started to look at Honolulu in detail, we found the specific zip codes that had a higher penetration of the target audience. We would advertise to people who live in those zip codes, and not to the rest of the city.

Another Way to Target: Search

What is the best indication that someone is interested in your product? When they tell you they are looking for it. This is what happens on search. If I type "cucumber wet wipes" into a search engine such as Google, the makers of cucumber wipes can be pretty sure I am in the market for them. This is why search data is so powerful. And with so many people using search to help make purchasing decisions these days, making sure they find your product or service on the search engines is absolutely vital. Bill Hunt, the founder of GSI (Global

Strategies Inc.), a Seattle-based company that specializes in search, wrote the industry textbook on how to optimize your online assets so they can be found on search engines. (The concept is known as "search engine optimization," or SEO.) Hunt's book *Search Engine Marketing Inc.* is well worth your time, as is *Search Engine Optimization: An Hour a Day* by Jennifer Grappone and Gradiva Couzin. Both are incredibly detailed and helpful. But for our purposes here, there are two ways to find someone via a search engine—organic search and paid search.

If I type in "cucumber wet wipes" in Google, I will get two types of information. The first is the organic search results that pop up as a result of my actual search. If you want your offering to pop up at the top of the list, you need to optimize the content of your site so the search engines will rank you the highest. This can be done in a number of ways, all of which are described in detail in *Search Engine Marketing Inc.*

In addition to the organic search results, there are the paid search results on the right or sometimes at the very top of the page. If I sell cucumber wet wipes I can buy these "search terms" from Google so that every time someone types in cucumber wet wipes, my ad will appear. This is what is called "paid search."

If you type in "cucumber wet wipes" on Google, you will see Boots is missing out by not advertising, and that could be a problem. For example, if all I remember is that my wife likes cucumber wipes, and the name of the brand she likes had something to do with shoes, I am never going to recall the name, and Boots won't get a sale.

Individual targeting. If we take a step back, we realize media planning and geo targeting are blunt instruments compared to targeting one specific individual. Search is a very good medium to try to reach the right individual at the right time, but we can't rely on the moment a consumer actively types the words into a search engine as the only method to find him. (What happens if he never searches, or if a competitor woos him before he ever sees our search ad?)

Given the shortcomings of the methods we have talked about so far, we need other ways of targeting consumers. Perhaps not surprisingly, this is where the majority of the technological advances have been made over the last few years. This information on specific individuals we are looking for tends to reside in three types of places:

- *Internal databases*, which store all the interactions consumers have with a company (e.g., in their stores, on their website, in their call center)

- *External databases*, which have information about consumers based on magazine subscriptions, email lists, the census, etc.

- *Digital networks*, which store browser interactions with digital assets across vast digital networks

Let's discuss each.

Internal Databases

For decades, companies have been building databases that capture all the information generated when customers interact with them. Tracking that data usually begins when a customer registers on a website or buys something. To show how it works, let's take what happens when you make a purchase from a retailer. Every time you swipe your card, the cash register creates a few lines in a log that can look like the figure on page 101.

time	date	store ID	SKU	price	retail price	transaction type	transaction ID	customer ID
3:01:22	3/23/10	1543	1293123	2.32	2.32	purchase	0000001	0000001
3:01:22	3/23/10	1543	7305629	4.65	4.65	purchase	0000001	0000001
3:01:22	3/23/10	1543	6492026	12.55	10.99	purchase	0000001	0000001
3:01:23	3/23/10	1543	7998272	3.99	3.99	purchase	0000001	0000001
3:01:26	3/23/10	1543	1111111	23.51	21.95	payment	0000001	0000001
3:42:18	3/23/10	1543	2234893	6.44	6.44	purchase	0000002	0000002
3:42:18	3/23/10	1543	8726032	8.98	8.98	purchase	0000002	0000002
3:42:18	3/23/10	1543	6253922	2.98	2.98	purchase	0000002	0000002
3:42:19	3/23/10	1543	6482334	24.87	22.99	purchase	0000002	0000002
3:42:19	3/23/10	1543	3940062	12.74	12.74	purchase	0000002	0000002
3:42:21	3/23/10	1543	1111111	56.01	54.13	payment	0000002	0000002
8:32:45	3/25/10	1543	1293123	2.32	2.32	purchase	0000098	0000001
8:32:45	3/25/10	1543	7305629	4.65	4.65	purchase	0000098	0000001
8:32:45	3/25/10	1543	6492026	12.55	10.99	purchase	0000098	0000001
8:32:47	3/25/10	1543	7998272	3.99	3.99	purchase	0000098	0000001
8:32:47	3/25/10	1543	7362932	4.98	4.98	purchase	0000098	0000001
8:32:52	3/25/10	1543	1111111	28.49	26.93	payment	0000098	0000001

This type of file usually captures the following items:

- *Time of purchase*
- *Date of purchase*
- *Store ID:* a number that indicates which store the transaction took place in
- *SKU:* Stockkeeping unit; a number that indicates which product was purchased
- *Price:* what the product cost
- *Actual price:* the price that was actually paid at the register (including any discounts given)
- *Transaction ID:* which line items are part of one transaction
- *Payment method:* whether the payment was made by cash, credit card, check, or whatever
- *Customer ID:* a number that indicates which customer is making the purchase

The last item, the customer ID, is the one that enables retailers to identify who is actually doing the buying. It enables them to target customers.

How do they know who you are? The mechanisms retailers put in place vary. Many offer loyalty cards that enable you to buy at a discount and/or generate points that can be redeemed for gifts. For the retailer, these cards do two things: First, they ·create stronger ties with the customer, since you will likely return to the retailer who rewards you to grow your points balance and get you more discounts. Second, and more important, it allows the retailer to know exactly what you bought. When you use the loyalty card, it automatically populates the customer ID field in the cash register log.

The other way some retailers link the transactions to individuals is through a credit card. When you charge something, the credit card company records it in order to bill you. This enables the company to work with the retailers to populate the customer ID field in the cash register log.

No matter which way it happens, once the retailer has learned what you bought, it can create a "single customer view," a view that captures all of the retailers' dealings with you in one place. There is no magic behind this. It's plain old common sense. First we would translate the file shown above into a new file that has one line per transaction.

It could look something like this:

time	date	store ID	price	retail price	nr products	transaction ID	customer ID
3:01:26	3/23/10	1543	23.51	21.95	4	0000001	0000001
3:42:21	3/23/10	1543	56.01	54.13	5	0000002	0000002
8:32:52	3/25/10	1543	28.49	26.93	5	0000098	0000001

This table can then be aggregated further to create a single customer view that has one line per customer.

customer ID	nr transactions	avg prod/ trans	avg price/ trans	date 1st purchase	date last purchase	total value
0000001	1	5	54.13	3/23/10	3/23/10	54.13
0000002	2	4.5	24.44	3/23/10	3/25/10	48.88

This file has a number of variables that describe the behavior of the customers 0000001 and 0000002:

- *number of transactions:* the total number of transactions during the time period
- *average product/transaction:* the average number of products bought per transaction

- *average price/transaction:* the average price paid per transaction
- *date of first purchase:* to show the length of the relationship with the customer
- *date of last purchase:* the date of the most recent purchase, indicating if this is a current customer
- *total value:* the sum of everything the customer bought, which gives the retailer an idea of how important the customer is to them

The single customer view can have many more data points (or columns, in the examples above) that can show:

- What products were purchased
- Where the customer lives
- The sociodemographic characteristics of the zip code where the customer lives
- Customer contact details, such as email address or mobile phone
- What marketing communications a customer has received and has responded to
- What other interactions the customer has had with the call center, the website (more on this in a second), or any other platform the company has

Capturing this information is one of the most common tasks performed by people doing data analytics. It is not limited to retailers. Telephone companies have similar databases. So do banks and airlines, which will also know where and how the booking was made and details about the routes chosen. The crucial data point in all of this is the customer ID, which allows companies to tie all that activity to an individual customer.

Information transacted on a company's website can also be included in the single customer view. To use my experience as an example, let's look at all the information I left behind simply by looking in on my favorite football ("soccer") team.

One morning I went to the BBC website to check on Arsenal,

which plays in the English Premier League. Here is what happened when I went online and typed www.bbc.co.uk/football into my browser. My computer rang the BBC web server, a big database that holds all the pages of the BBC website. My computer has a telephone number associated with it—well, not really a telephone number. It's called an IP address. But it works the same way. Your computer has a unique IP address, just like your unique phone number, that the websites you visit can easily capture. So the BBC now knows I requested the football (using the correct term for soccer now) pages from its server.

IP addresses are one way of identifying people online when they surf. But it turns out there are some problems with using IP addresses as an identifier. The main problem is caused by something called proxy servers. Let's say, for example, that I went to the BBC site from work. It would not be my laptop's IP address dialing the BBC server; it would be my work computer's address. And because of the way the network at work is set up, everyone at Ogilvy in NewYork dials in from the same IP address. So the BBC would actually not see my individual computer; it would only see which network I am connected to. This is a lot less useful to them. This also happens very often. Just think about how often you surf the web from work.

To solve this issue someone invented the *cookie*. Here is what happens when cookies are involved when I surf the web. I go to the BBC site from my computer. The BBC server will send me the pages I asked for, but it will also send me a little text file, a cookie, which it will put in a folder on my hard drive.

The next time I visit the BBC website, the BBC server will not only send me the pages I asked for, it will also read my BBC cookie, which tells them it is my computer asking for these pages, even if I am dialing in from a different network. It will update the cookie to reflect that I visited the site again and will also capture the pages I view.

The approach is not perfect, of course. Consumers can easily delete cookies from their computer. If I did that, and then returned to the BBC site, the server would think I was a new visitor. Of course, the problem with people deleting cookies, from a marketer's point of view, is that there is no way to target the customer individually.

I have a feeling that in the near future we are going to be talking about cookies the same way we now discuss the Model T. There are more detailed techniques on the horizon. A company called BlueCava is "fingerprinting" computers and mobile devices worldwide. You might think that one computer is basically like another, but it turns out that is not the case, as the *Wall Street Journal* pointed out in writing about BlueCava: "Each computer has a different clock setting, different fonts, different software and many other characteristics that make it unique. Every time a typical computer goes online, it broadcasts hundreds of such details as a calling card to other computers it communicates with. Tracking companies can use this data to uniquely identify computers, cellphones and other devices, and then build profiles of the people who use them."

That, of course, would allow advertisers to target you directly. It would also allow them to target different devices differently. This will become more important in the future. People are using different devices in different ways. I use my laptop more for work and my iPad for recreation. If someone wants to target me with sports-related content, it would be better to do so on my iPad.

Another way to reach customers directly is through a technology known as "deep packet inspection" (sometimes referred to as deep packet sniffing). It can read and analyze all the bits, or packets, of data that travel across the web. Because it can track all information, not just web browsing, you can see how it can be much more effective than a cookie in compiling information about an individual.

The third way websites can currently identify you is through registration. This is how Amazon.com works. Once I register my username and password, Amazon knows it is me making the requests for pages from their site every time I come back. They can then gather and analyze the data in very much the same way as the companies that offer loyalty cards do.

You can also link a person's surfing behavior to his offline behavior in the store. Here's how it works. Say I have registered on the Sears website and spend a lot of time looking at garden furniture. If I then go to my local Sears store and purchase a new patio table and chairs with my Sears credit card, Sears can trace back the sale to the fact that I looked at the website. The concept is known as ROBO: research online, buy offline. It is one way the people in online marketing justify their budgets and track which offers are working.

Registration is the most accurate way of capturing an individual. It would get it right even if multiple people were using one computer (something a cookie wouldn't pick up), because each time you visit the Amazon site you are asked if you are a returning customer. Registration online is the only way a company will be able to know which physical person is surfing its website.

You Can Capture Even More Data

I am sure you have noticed the commonality in everything we have talked about so far. It is all about capturing data on the platforms you control—your website, your cash register, your phone network —to allow you to create a single customer view that will help you talk to your customer. But it's possible to get even more data than that.

External Databases

Some data is for sale. There is an entire industry that sells data to companies eager to get smarter about who they target. The United States and the United Kingdom have the most sophisticated suppliers. In the United States, the credit score companies make data available so that marketers can not only see where you spend your money but also how good you are at paying it back. In addition, there is the sociodemographic data I mentioned earlier—information about who lives in certain zip codes, for example—that is provided by the Census Bureau of the United States.

Companies such as Claritas have combined that data with other sources to build detailed profiles of zip codes. They have translated these profiles into archetypal segments (see our discussion in Chapter 3), which are mapped to each zip code.

Again, there is nothing new about this type of data; it has been around for years. I wanted to mention it to underscore that while you certainly want to pay attention to all the new tools that are coming along, you don't want to ignore what has always worked.

Then there are the compiled lists, comprised of data you leave behind when you subscribe to a book club, magazine, newsletter, wine-of-the-month club, and the like. (You always have the ability to prevent companies from passing on your information to someone else, but this is usually mentioned in the fine print.)

Finding people on external lists can be incredibly powerful. For one thing, it allows you to discover what your customer likes (beyond the things she purchases from you), which can suggest other things you can sell to her. (She likes fine wine, and you are a department store. You can target her for upscale wineglasses.)

LIST NAME	TOTAL LIST UNIVERSE	GENDER	LIST DESCRIPTION
Active Network Masterfile	15,000,000	55% MALE	As part of the Active Network, the leading provider of software and technology solutions for participatory sports and activities, we work with thousands of facilities and events each year to power the things people love to do. This gives us an unprecedented access to consumers who are participating in their favorite activities, including running, soccer, golf, yoga, lacrosse and over 80 other sports activities and events.
Athleta	395,851	16% MALE	Specializing in women's sports and casual apparel and accessories. Athleta is an industry-leading outfitter that offers only the best selection of high-quality performance and propriety brand products. The Athleta woman purchases fitness and outdoor-related apparel that enables her to push herself every day to exceed her goals
Bass Pro Shops Catalogue Buyers	1,166,958	83% MALE	Bass Pro Shops catalog buyers enjoy the outdoors in every way. Their interests range from hunting and fishing to camping and hiking, to cooking and water sports. The Bass Pro Shops catalogue features an array of quality products designed to help them meet the needs of their active lifestyles, with a complete selection of hunting, fishing, campging and marine gear, plus rugged apparel and footwear, outdoor furniture and cookware, even unique gifts for the home or cabin.
Campmor Inc	323,524	53% MALE	CAMPMOR mail order buyers are young, ages 26–45, with an average income of $60,000. These buyers are dedicated to their outdoor activities and the environment. CAMPMOR is the leading source for quality outdoor equipment, gear and clothing products for both adults and children. Products purchased include tents, camping equipment, climbing and skiing gear, bicycles, etc.
Champion	175,866	20% MALE	Champion excites the interest of sports enthusiasts everywhere ... with best-selling athletic apparel for men, women and kids. It's the largest assortment of Champion apparel anywhere ... from world-famous hoodies and sports bras to high-performance workout wear to comfortable, versatile active wear. http://www.championusa.com
Duluth Trading Company	492,265	63% MALE	The Duluth Trading Co. catalogue is an essential tool for all outdoor enthusiasts and rugged craftsman and -women. The slim jim catalogue is loaded with hardworking durable apparel, footwear, boots, jackets, gloves, tools and accessories, gadgets, gifts, travel books and gear as well as various related general merchandise items. This demanding audience age 45+ is willing to spend to get their hands on top-quality long-lasting products offered in the Duluth Trading Co. catalogue and website.
Eddie Bauer Catalogue Buyers	1,415,125	22% MALE	The Eddie Bauer catalogue features high-quality men's and women's apparel and has earned a reputation as America's premier outfitter. They also carry a variety of home furnishings field hardware, domestics, etc. The median age of the Eddie Bauer customer is 42; median household income is $91K; 74% are highly educated. http://www.eddiebauer.com
Eddie Bauer Internet Buyers	781,704	24% MALE	Reach Eddie Bauer customers who love the convenience of shopping on the Internet. These internet at postal buyers have an average age of 47 and an average household income of $74K; 74% are highly educated. http://www.eddiebauer.com

You can also find prospects who aren't in your internal database. Here is an example. We were working with a department store that had just introduced a new line of sporting goods with lots of excellent products. However, people don't traditionally think of department stores when it comes to high-end sporting goods, so a big chunk of the target audience wasn't shopping with the store. Finding sporting-goods buyers on external lists became crucial. So we scanned the market for what was available. The chart on page 108 is just the first page of our final recommendation about all the lists the client should use, along with a description of the lists provided by the stores that are selling the names of their customers.

This exercise allowed us to find 10 million sporting equipment and/or apparel buyers who made a purchase in the category in the previous twelve months. This is a great example of how you can find a big audience for what you are selling through lists that are commercially available.

Targetable panels are another source for finding the right individuals. They can, as noted earlier, be very useful to discovering the profile of a specific group. This is the way television ratings work. Nielsen creates a panel of people who represent the population as a whole, and then monitors their TV consumption. Most panels are anonymous, and can't be targeted.

Those panels that are targetable present a great opportunity for companies such as packaged-goods producers that don't know who buys their soft drinks, milk, bread, and soap. But retailers, such as supermarkets, do—thanks to the loyalty cards they offer. Kantar Retail, a marketing research firm, has partnered with a wide range of retailers and gets the shopping information they collect through loyalty cards. Kantar then merges the data from all these retailers to build their enormous panel of 80 million US households. For each of those households, they know what brands they bought, when, and how often. They also know what else was in the shopping basket. The only thing they don't know is the name and address of the person. That is kept anonymous to respect privacy. Kantar works with a neutral third party who takes the retailer's information—which does have the name and address—appends a blind ID (a number that is unique to the household), and then passes on the shopping behavior with the blind ID (without the name and address) to Kantar Retail. This way the folks at Kantar Retail can't look up their neighbors to see what they purchased!

Still, having access to this data is extremely powerful. The department store, for example, could go into the panel and identify anyone who has an above-average consumption of sports drinks and who lives in the vicinity of one of its stores. This could give them a very specific group to go after. They could pass on the blind IDs to the neutral party, who would then match it to the physical name and address. This enables companies that work with Kantar to target small segments of customers who are very similar in terms of their shopping behavior in retail stores.

Digital Networks

We've shown how to use internal and external databases to find individual potential customers and how to find where large groups of people are spending time online. Now, let's see how you can target a specific individual online.

Let's say an online brokerage knows that people who go to CNNMoney.com are more likely to be receptive to an offer to use their services. But not everyone who visits CNNMoney is a target. So how does the brokerage decide which people to show their banner ad to on the CNNMoney website and which people to exclude? Since the company must pay CNNMoney a fee every time the banner appears, this is a very important question.

The answer is where individual level targeting comes into play online, and it is one of the most exciting areas in marketing today. It's a place where the number of technological innovations is staggering. To fully answer the question, let's take a step back.

The online brokerage can get its banner on CNNMoney in two ways. The first is to contact CNN directly and ask to purchase a number of impressions—i.e., an ad that appears on the website a specific number of times. The second option is to go through an ad network (a broker) that matches the demand for ad placements from the financial services companies of the world (the advertisers) with the available ad placements (the inventory) on the websites of the CNNs out there (the publishers).

While this is pretty straightforward, it soon gets a lot more interesting. Early on, the ad networks understood the value of everyone who visited a website. They started recording every time they sent an ad to a person surfing the web. As a result, they know that a certain banner was shown at a certain place at a certain time to a certain person. That transaction log looked very similar to the website databases or transactional logs described earlier. And by sending a cookie, they could keep track of everyone who actually clicked on the ad. This allows the ad networks to follow people across multiple websites.

Say you went to Site #1, which uses an ad network to place online ads on its site. Let's say the ad network shows you an ad for blue jeans. The ad network would attach a cookie to your computer noting what banner you looked at and whether you clicked on it.

Let's say you clicked on the banner but you didn't like the jeans you were shown and you headed over to another retail site and looked at sweaters. If Site #2 is a member of the same ad network as Site #1, it will recognize the cookie on your computer and may very well present you with an ad for a different style of blue jeans. This explains why a certain ad can follow you from site to site.

Google, Yahoo!, and Microsoft, owners of the biggest networks, obviously also own the biggest search engines. They have created databases that show what everyone visited; what ads they saw; and, of course, what people searched for. What would that tell you about a person's likelihood to click on a banner ad or even purchase your product? You got it: a lot. When a potential advertiser says it wants to reach people who have an interest in the finer things in life (because they are good prospects), the ad networks make sure that the appropriate people see those ads. The smarter the ad networks get at targeting their ads, the higher the performance of the ads and the more money advertisers will spend on the ad network. This is why the sexy little numbers are big business for the Googles, Microsofts and Yahoo!s of the world.

Now here's where it gets interesting. If I am the online brokerage, I will pay more to show my banner to someone with a high likelihood of becoming a client of mine. How much would I pay? Actually, you could do the math yourself. It's a pretty easy calculation.

$$A = (P(C) \times MC) / ROI$$

A is the allowable (maximum) price the brokerage is prepared to pay to show its ad to a certain person. $P(C)$ is the probability that person will convert to become a client. MC is the margin per conversion, the profit the brokerage makes if that person becomes a client. ROI is the return on investment the company expects from what it spends. If it expects a three-to-one ROI, then the price the company is prepared to pay (A) will be lower than if they expect a two-to-one ROI.

Companies usually have a pretty good idea of what MC

is and what ROI they need. The key number in the equation on page 112 is P(C), the likelihood someone will convert. Wouldn't it be great if you could calculate the P(C) and the allowable for every cookie out there and then pay only for the ones you can get below your allowable? Absolutely. Let's see how you would do it.

As an example, let's say you and I both go to ESPN.com tomorrow. I like computer games; you don't. EA Sports is bringing out a new basketball game, which they will be advertising online. Suppose they can see you browsing ESPN.com and they have the opportunity to place their ad at the top of the page. To do that will cost them 5 cents. (In reality, it probably costs them more like 0.003 cents, or about $3 for 1,000 impressions—i.e., ads—but let's use 5 cents to keep the math simple and to keep you from having a calculator at your side as you read along.) But they know you have never been to a gamer site, that you have seen some of their ads but haven't clicked on them, and that you only visit the ESPN home page and the pages on golf. Your P(C) will be pretty low. If they calculate the A for you, it would be below 5 cents.

The wise decision would be to save money by not showing you the ad—since the odds are remote you would buy a game—and to use that money on someone like me, someone who they know clicked on one of their banners for a soccer game not all that long ago, someone who they could also see frequently visits the basketball pages on ESPN and who they know searched for New York Knicks tickets in the past. EA Sports would be better off spending its five cents on me.

Now a nickel (or the real figure of $3 per 1,000 impressions) might not sound like a lot of money, but imagine this happening over millions of advertising impressions every day and you see the power of being able to target the actual individual versus everyone who happens to visit ESPN.com. The benefits are obvious; and today companies are able to target their online advertising this way. Two things have happened to make this possible: the birth of advertising exchanges and the emergence of real-time bidding.

Ad exchanges are auction-based marketplaces for ad inventory. They bring together publishers (ESPN in the example above) and buyers (EA Sports in the same example), and they are designed to make the whole buying and selling process more fluid, simpler, and efficient through the use of technology.

The major ad exchanges are AdECN, owned by Microsoft; Right Media, owned by Yahoo!; CONTEXTWEB Ad Exchange, the leading independent exchange; and DoubleClick Ad Exchange, owned by Google. The power of ad exchanges really comes to life through real-time bidding (RTB).

The concept of RTB is pretty straightforward. Let's take the example we used before, of you and I visiting the ESPN.com page. To keep things simple, let's say EA is a potential bidder and so is the car company BMW, since your visits to the ESPN.com golf pages has driven up your P(C) as far as BMW is concerned. We both type in "ESPN.com," and the ad server recognizes who we are. Because you are potentially more valuable to them than I am, BMW is willing to pay more than EA to make sure you see their car ad. My allowable for EA Sports is higher than what BMW is prepared to pay for me. EA Sports wins the bid, and I will see an ad for the EA basketball game. All of this happens in a fraction of a second.

Now, it isn't EA and BMW themselves who are calculating how much they are willing to pay per impression. Odds are, they have hired an outside firm to do the math (based on the parameters they've set). These specialty vendors not only calculate the allowable, using some of the algorithms I described earlier, but they also make a prediction about what others are going to be prepared to pay for a particular impression. These are the types of algorithms Wall Street brokers use to pick stocks. And recently the rocket scientists who wrote the algorithms for Wall Street have started to write them for the ad exchanges. One former actual rocket scientist who now does this for a living told me the trick is to predict what the second-highest bid would be and then bid just a fraction higher. This makes a lot of sense.

Let's use our BMW/EA example (and oversimplified math) again to show how this could work. If BMW's allowable for showing you the ad on ESPN.com is 10 cents, but they know that the second highest bid is going to be a nickel, they are far better off bidding 5.5 cents than a dime. Companies that master this approach will be able to save an awful lot of money while still targeting the people it is best for them to go after.

Winning this game comes down to two things: mastering the math and getting access to data about cookies. The more information you have about the cookies, the better the math will work, and the more money you will make by bidding for the right cookies. This is how data equals money in digital space and this is why the collection, management, and analysis of this data is big business. Companies such as BlueKai are specializing in building data management platforms (DMPs) that will help their clients do just this. This is one of the fastest-growing areas in the marketing world today.

I mentioned that Google, Yahoo!, and Microsoft own the biggest ad networks. Now Apple is getting into the game as well. Imagine what they know about your preferences if you use iTunes. The music, movies, and apps people like can reveal a lot about what other products they could be interested in. So Apple has developed an advertising solution called iAd. It allows advertisers to target iTunes users on their Apple devices, with ads based on everything known about how these users use iTunes.

And we are not only talking about banner ads. The iPad allows advertisers to create entire immersive advertising experiences (more engaging than even the best TV ads) and target customers with pinpoint accuracy. Here's an example. We did a highly successful iPad campaign for Perrier in France that invited the user into a virtual burlesque-like world with beautiful women in lingerie (obviously a much more engaging experience than a simple print ad).

When we launched the ad, our Perrier clients complained they couldn't see it when they surfed the web on their iPads. It took us a long time to convince them that we really did run the ad, but that it was so targeted that it was shown only to high-potential individuals, and that somehow they weren't part of that group—maybe because they got their Perrier for free.

This is a far different game from the world of TV, where everyone gets to see the ad. No wonder iAd has advertisers super excited.

Looking in Other Places

So far I have talked only about online advertising. But there are other digital networks where you can find people who might be worth targeting. Social networks have become one of the most important ones. In the examples used so far, all the data involved the places people visited, what they were exposed to, and what they interacted with. Imagine what Facebook, Foursquare, Twitter, and MySpace know about their users. They know not only about your interests *but also about those of your friends.* Imagine how predictive that data is about what you like and who else might be interested in the products you like. This area is very much in its infancy. And it isn't surprising that companies like Facebook have been valued at more than $50 billion. They have the ability to deliver very specific targets to advertisers. They say to advertisers: "We can find just about any potential target you want by age, geography, income, interests, etc. You tell us who you are looking for and give us your ad message, and we will deliver it to them—for a fee."

Facebook has even developed advertising that comes with an endorsement from your friends. The folks at Facebook know that the effectiveness of an ad endorsed by your friends is much higher than one that simply comes to you out of the blue. In fact, Brad Smallwood, head of analytics at Facebook, told me that a friend's endorsement increased purchasing intent by a factor of four! That shouldn't surprise us.

What does this mean for targeting? A lot. At the time I spoke to Brad, the fan page for the North Face clothing company had 482,000 fans. And these fans had a total of 51.9 million friends. This means that North Face could target those 51.9 million people with an ad on Facebook that has their friends' endorsement on it—an ad that would be four times more effective if they placed it elsewhere without the friends' endorsements.

How people influence each other has been the subject of quite a lot of interesting academic research. Social networks provide academics with the perfect lab to investigate how information gets disseminated throughout networks, as David Huffaker's work points out.

David is an expert in social media analytics, an exciting and relatively new field. He has analyzed behavior on social networks such as Google Groups, Google's former social media platform, to get a better understanding of how influencers (he refers to them as "leaders") behave. He identified these people based on three criteria:

1. Does the content they create trigger replies?

2. Do these replies generate conversations?

3. Do the followers adopt the influencer's language in these conversations?

His findings were not surprising but interesting nevertheless. He learned that:

- *Leaders are active.* They are more likely to post messages, reply to others, and have a longer tenure in the community.

- *Leaders are social.* They rely more on replying to others than merely on broadcasting.

- *Leaders are passionate.* They will demonstrate higher frequencies of talkativeness, affective language (they use words such as good, bad, love, hate . . .), assertiveness (use of words such as *always* and *never*), and linguistic diversity.

In coming years you can expect an inordinate amount of research to be done to determine what is the ROI of reaching these people. In fact, it is already under way, as Eric Sun's work shows.

Eric wanted to know how information flows through Facebook, so he did an analysis of 262,985 Facebook pages and their associated fans.

The accepted wisdom is that the popularity of a page starts with a small number of important influencers who then sway their large networks. But Sun learned that it is more important to find a large population on Facebook than it is to find a small number of influentials. The Facebook network is very connected. Because of this, good ideas will attract wide, long, connected clusters of people.

As you can see from these two bits of research, when it comes to social networks, not only do you have to worry about who to target, you must also take into account how your message will be spread to others. And from a quick look at the research Huffaker and Sun have done, you can immediately imagine how useful the data gathered on social networks can be in deciding whom to target. What someone says she likes, how social she is, how active she is, and with whom she is friends—all can be very powerful data points for any company looking to determine the allowable and the P(C) of a user on a social network.

Another social targeting platform, 33Across, is helping companies be more effective in reaching social networks. The company focuses on the connections people have with each other and the influence those connections have on things like brand preference and likability. Its founder, Eric Wheeler, used to work at Ogilvy. For the last few years Eric has been building the largest *social graph* out there. A social graph is the mapping of everyone and how we interact with one another through various social media such as Facebook. Eric's database contains cookie information for over 200 million people, all of it completely anonymous in order to protect consumer privacy.

Advertisers use 33Across to build *brand graphs.* The graphs show the company's most loyal users—based on purchasing data—and then companies might target people who are linked to those customers through various social media. Why target those people? Because historical research suggests that we buy and like the same things as the people we are connected to.

The precision with which you can target on these types of networks is incredible. But soon you will be able to use all media—even your television set—to target efficiently. It is already possible technologically. In the United States,

Cablevision has already made addressable TV a reality for three million households in the New York region. For these households, marketers are able to target individual set-top boxes with ads based on everything they know about the households. Dish Network and DirecTV are currently implementing similar technology that will enable marketers to target 15 million households in the United States through their set-top boxes. This means you and your neighbor could be watching the same TV program but receiving different ads based on your profile.

Michael Bologna at WPP's GroupM is one of the world's experts in the area of addressable TV. He always reminds me how wasteful TV really is. It's a very blunt instrument. For example, to target mothers with kids under 10 years old, you would usually end up buying the women 18–49 segment. You would pay anywhere between $12 and $18 to reach a thousand women 18–49. Now, a lot of those women will not have kids. So let's look at how much you really pay to reach women with kids under 10. You would really be paying $25 to $35 to reach a thousand of them. The rest of your spending would be wasted. Addressable TV, on the other hand, would allow you to target only women with kids under 10. You might pay $20 to reach a thousand of them, which may seem more expensive than the initial $12 to $18; but because you know you will be talking only to women with children under 10, you are actually paying a lot less for your target.

Michael believes that over the next few years we will be able to reach 30–40 million households through addressable TV. The potential is enormous. And it will fundamentally change the way media is bought, because advertisers will start applying the techniques of digital and direct targeting we described earlier in this chapter to TV advertising.

THINGS TO DO MONDAY MORNING

1. *Can they find you?* Sure, you want to be able to target the right people, but sometimes they come looking for you. The first thing I would do on Monday morning is start optimizing the chances that your company's name and products jump to the top of the list, when someone is searching online for what you have to sell. (Start by picking up the two books on search engine optimization I mentioned earlier in this chapter.)

2. *Where do you start looking for them?* You can't, of course, rely only on folks looking for you, so you will need proactively to try and reach your customers. Where you start depends on how much you have to spend and where you want to spend it (the next chapter will help you figure that out). But if you are spending on broad-based media, you want to make sure that whatever you found out about your target audience is reflected in your media plan. I would sit down with your media partner and have him walk you through why he selected certain media. Have him show you the numbers. You know what they mean now.

3. *For a lot of smaller companies, broad-based media is not really an option.* That is not a problem. Individual level targeting can be extremely powerful. Try and mine your internal databases first. Then explore some of the external databases we discussed. And make sure you explore digital and social networks. The cost is extremely reasonable.

CHAPTER FIVE

BUDGET: "HOW MUCH SHOULD WE SPEND?"

By now we know who we want to talk to; we know what we want to talk about; and we know where to find these people so we can hold that conversation.

Now the big question is, how much money will we spend communicating with our customers and prospects? Whether the number ends up being big or small, this chapter is designed to make sure you get the absolutely highest return from your marketing investment. That will put you ahead of most of your competitors.

As you are about to read, most companies don't use a lot of science in deciding how much to spend on marketing—and that's true whether they spend a few thousand or a few hundred million dollars a year.

My focus in this chapter is twofold: to help you determine what your marketing budget should be—showing you the best way to figure out what to spend to create demand—and then, once you have that number, how to allocate your funds by task, geography, and channel.

If I had a dollar for every time I have been asked the question in the chapter title—how much should we spend?—I would have a very pleasant second income. How much to spend is a question on every marketer's mind these days. And that doesn't surprise me. For way too long, folks have been spending a lot of money—in the case of the packaged goods companies, literally billions of dollars each year—without really knowing what they get for it in return. That's just silly. As a politician once said, "A billion here, a billion there. Pretty soon we're talking about real money." In 2012 companies are expected to spend $154 billion in advertising in the United States alone.

Let's assume that a more rigorous approach would result in just a 1 percent improvement in effectiveness. This means that companies would be able to generate $1.5 billion in incremental value. With so much at stake, it's not surprising that much has been written about how to figure out how much to spend. Some thirty years ago, Harry Henry published an article in *The Cranfield Broadsheet*, from the Cranfield University School of Management in the United Kingdom, that described fifteen approaches determing how to spend. These are:

1. *Intuitive/rule of thumb.* Enough to do the job based on experience.

2. *Maintaining previous spend.* Keep doing what you have been doing—if it is working. (Sometimes the figure is adjusted for inflation.)

3. *Percent of previous sales.* Backward looking, rewards success (or compounds failure).

4. *Affordable.* What fits within the budget?

5. *Residue of last year's profits.* This approach focuses on the source of funds, not their use.

6. *Percent of gross margin* . . . which begs the question of cost efficiency.

7. *Percent of forecast sales.* The most common method.

8. *Fixed cost per unit of sales.* The arithmetic is simple.

9. *Cost per customer/capita.* This approach is often found among those companies that sell business-to-business.

10. *Match what competitors are spending* . . . which of course, assumes competitors know what they are doing.

11. *Match "share of voice" to brand share.* If you have 5 percent of the market, you spend 5 percent of what the entire market spends on advertising.

12. *Marginal return.* Only possible in direct response. You keep expanding your audience until the estimated incremental return of the additional target is lower than your target return.

13. *Task approach.* You define your objectives and cost out how to reach them. (Best in theory but may require extensive econometric modeling to determine.)

14. *Modeling.* The most sophisticated approach (and therefore not easy).

15. *Media weight tests.* You go out in the marketplace and spend money in one place (say the East Coast) and not in another (the West Coast) and then compare the results. It sounds simple, but it is usually difficult to evaluate or replicate.

And nothing much has changed over the last thirty years. Most marketers just pick one of the fifteen methods listed above, with the research showing—and my own experience confirms this—that marketing as a percentage of sales is the most popular approach. I am often surprised by how frequently simple, crude, and not very accurate rules like these are used by some of the biggest companies in the world to make decisions on how to create huge advertising budgets.

There are more scientific methods, such as the last two in Harry Henry's list. And the funny thing is, most have been around for decades. However, companies seem to struggle to incorporate them in the decision making process. Science is often seen as a black box—too hard to understand. As a result, I have even seen companies that invest heavily in science to create their products—such as the pharmaceutical industry—revert to very basic rules, such as advertising as a percentage of sales, when the actual marketing budgeting decisions were being made. This is a real shame. The fact that rules such as advertising as a percentage of sales are easier to explain doesn't mean they are better for decision making.

And it certainly doesn't mean that they should replace more scientific approaches.

There is no single best approach to budget setting. But let's look at a few of the best. We'll begin by looking at spend/get curves.

THE SPEND/GET CURVE

The response curve below shows what you get for your money when it comes to marketing—what I often refer to as a *spend/ get curve*. The *spend* is the marketing investment and the *get* is what you are trying to achieve with that investment—for example, an increase in sales or profits, or branding objectives such as building awareness or consideration. The figure below is a typical response curve for brand awareness.

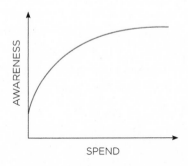

Let's look at this simple curve more closely:

- The slope of the curve is positive. This indicates that the more you spend on awareness, the higher awareness will be.

- The curve shows decreasing marginal returns. This means that, depending on what your current spending and awareness levels are, you will get different returns. As you can see, the higher the current spend, the less you will get from shelling out additional money. What follows from that is, you could ultimately reach a saturation point where you will get no increased incremental awareness from boosting your spending. (You see that at the far right of the curve.)

These kinds of curves are very intuitive. The difficulty usually lies in constructing them. If historical data on spend and awareness levels is available, scientific approaches such as econometric modeling can make life a lot easier by estimating the slope and shape of the response curves. That, of course, raises the question: What is econometric modeling?

SCIENCE: ECONOMETRIC Models

At the University of Antwerp I majored in quantitative economics, an area that relies heavily on math. Not surprisingly, it wasn't a popular major. People who liked math tended to major in engineering or science, not economics. So it was only the very few who weren't scared of math, and who didn't want to be engineers, who ended up in quantitative economics. That isn't an exaggeration. Of the 1,000 students in my class, there were only 6 quant econ majors. This meant classes in my major subject were normally a lot more interactive than in other fields. It wasn't unusual, for example, to have 200 psychology majors in one room.

I say "normally" more interactive, because there was one glaring exception: my professor of econometrics. Econometrics is all about developing and applying *quantitative* or *statistical* methods to prove economic principles, and it is one of the most important classes quantitative economics majors take. The professor, who was close to retirement, was a brilliant econometrician but had never learned how to communicate in a classroom. In an auditorium designed to hold five hundred people—we never did figure out the scheduling snafu that had us meeting there—he stood in front of the six of us and mumbled. In the beginning, the six of us would sit in the first row, close to the podium, but he never acknowledged us; never made eye contact. When we decided to spread out across the entire auditorium one day, he didn't flinch and delivered another one of his trademark ninety-minute-long mumblings.

So, not surprisingly, my enthusiasm for econometrics was pretty low in the beginning, as was my grasp of how it could actually be applied. This changed dramatically in my last year at the university, when I was taught by some very interesting professors. One became responsible for economic policies of the Belgian government; he explained how econometrics could be used to forecast demand and supply in the economy so that proactive policy actions could be taken. Another showed how econometrics and other quantitative techniques could be used in marketing and sales. If it wasn't for her (and maybe also because of the small crush I had on her), I wouldn't have been able to write this book!

So how does econometric modeling work? Well, it is a technique that attempts to estimate the impact of a whole range of things on something else. That something else is usually total consumption or demand for products. In marketing, econometricians tend to look at demand for brands.

What could influence that demand? The price, quality, distribution, advertising, and just about anything else you think the demand for your products could be *a function of.* This literally tends to be expressed as a function, a mathematical one, such as a linear regression. (We have to get technical just for a minute. Don't worry. It won't last long and it is more intuitive than you might think.) A basic linear regression looks like this:

$$\text{Sales} = \beta_1 \times \text{supply} + \beta_2 \times \text{distribution} + \beta_3 \times \text{price} + \beta_4 \times \text{marketing} + \beta_5$$

β in each case is *beta*, or the unknown, as in What effect could supply have on the demand for what you have to sell? What effect could distribution have?, etc. If supply has a big impact, it has a high beta. If distribution really doesn't have that much impact, its beta is low.

You know what your supply, distribution, price, and marketing efforts are. Once you know the value of the β's, you know how these factors are driving sales. So the trick, as you have already figured out, is to estimate the β's. How does econometric modeling do that?

Let's take an example and, as you will see, the reason you may want to do this work is that it allows you to chart cause and effect as very simple graphs. And anything that can reduce complexity is a good thing.

Say we want to understand the impact of marketing efforts on sales for two brands, all other things being equal (i.e., supply, distribution, price, etc.). In this case, we are trying to find out what effect differing market expenditures have on sales over time. The graphs below show what these data points could look like for both brands. On the vertical axis, you have the sales of the brands. On the horizontal axis, you have the marketing efforts. Every dot is an observation—a certain spend and the associated sales level.

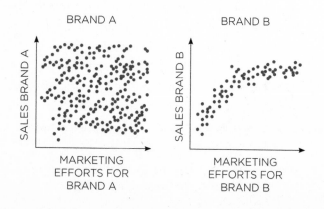

We see two very different pictures. For Brand A, there seems to be very little relationship between marketing efforts and sales. Each level of marketing spend has generated a whole range of different sales levels. In math terms, if we go back to our formula (Sales = $\beta 4 \times$ marketing), then β would probably be insignificant (in the statistical meaning of the word, there would be no significant correlation).

This is certainly not the case with Brand B. There we do see a relationship. Econometric modeling would be able to find the relationship between marketing and sales. It would do this by drawing an awareness curve that best fits the cloud of dots. Visually, we can see that the top line fits the cloud better than the bottom one.

So far, so good. But we don't want to have to draw these lines every time by hand; besides, not every situation is as simple as this. We need to be able to teach a computer to draw these kinds of lines so that it can find (real) patterns when we can't.

Here's how to do it. We tell the computer to calculate the distance between every dot and the line. Then we ask it to add up all those distances. The sum of these distances then indicates how good the fit is. The higher the sum, the worse the fit. That's how a computer can figure out which line fits the cloud best.

Now that it knows what to do, it can draw hundreds of lines

and pick out the one with the smallest sum, which is the one with the best fit. It can also do that for Sales vs. Price, Sales vs. Distribution, etc. In fact, we can—and should—ask it to create spend/get curves for every variable that affects sales.

Once we know all the curves we want to create, we can ask the computer to find the optimal point on each curve, that is, exactly how much we can spend to get the greatest possible return on our marketing investment and not a dollar more.

As you can see, econometric modeling is a relatively complex activity, one that is usually performed by expensive specialists. This can make it inaccessible to a lot of companies. But even firms that use econometrics often struggle to incorporate it into the decision-making process and on many occasions revert to simplistic rules such as advertising-to-sales ratios or adjusting last year's budget for inflation. Why? Because they don't understand econometrics or the underlying assumptions on which it is based. As a result, they prefer the simple rules mentioned above, since they are more intuitive and easier to explain—even though they really aren't based on anything real.

To address the concerns both of companies that cannot afford to do econometric modeling and of those who don't understand it, let's discuss some alternatives.

Art (A Hybrid Approach)

My ex-colleague David Coppock introduced me to the hybrid approach. David, who has a PhD in economics from Yale, was building complicated econometric models when I was playing with Lego blocks back in kindergarten.

David's approach uses econometrics where the data is available and fills in the gaps with assumptions when it is not. Once you have the mix of data and estimates, David's hybrid approach simply requires you to answer four questions:

- *Minimum:* In the awareness curve on page 129, what would the awareness level be if we didn't spend on awareness at all (far left of the curve)?

- *Maximum:* What awareness levels could we reach if we had an unlimited budget (far right of the curve)?

- *Current:* What are our current spending and awareness levels?

- *Incremental:* What do we think our awareness would be if we were to increase/decrease our spending by X percent?

I often use the hybrid approach to build response curves for clients. Sometimes there is resistance initially because they think the approach is "unscientific." The concern is that too many assumptions need to be made to construct the curves. This is not necessarily true. In this hybrid process, we always use whatever data or econometric models are available. However, in the absence of perfect data, assumptions will always need to be made.

In fact, if you were to revert to very crude rules such as advertising-to-sales ratios, you would be making far more assumptions about the relationship between spending and what you get in return for it. For example, you would be assuming that advertising has the same effect in promoting differing products; you would be assuming that content of the ad doesn't matter; you would be assuming the effect of advertising is linear—if spending $1 in advertising will produce $2 in sales, then spending $10 will produce $20—and so forth. So you can see why I think rules of thumb are *not* the way to go and the hybrid approach (when you have insufficient data) *is*.

There are three main advantages of using this hybrid approach to building response curves:

1. *You have the ability to mix hard data with judgment and intuition.* Take an unusual marketing campaign, such as the recent one for Dove that shows real women—i.e., women who didn't have perfect shapes—talking about their bodies and how much they loved Dove. Hard data might indicate that an ad campaign that tested well, as the Dove one did, would return $1.50 in sales for every $1 you spent. But you know from experience that ads like this, which really resonate with the market—as the qualitative research for this one confirmed—will do even better, so you adjust the spend/get graphs to show $1.70 coming in for every $1 you spend.

2. *Once response curves are built (using econometrics, assumptions, or a combination of both), they can be used for more scientific optimization.* For example, you can simply import the curve into an Excel spreadsheet and play with the variables to make more accurate projections.

3. *The process can be very open and collaborative—decision makers understand what is in the black box and are therefore more inclined to use the recommendations in decision making.* This is because they understand where the data comes from; i.e., they understand the information that makes up the spend/get curves.

Using this hybrid approach can take some of the mystery out of econometric modeling.

SETTING BUDGETS DURING A RECESSION

Our assumption in this chapter has been that marketing dollars will be relatively easy to come by. But what should you spend when times are hard? I remember very well when the recession hit in September 2008. I played a small part in our winning a big account that promptly disappeared. Let me explain.

In the summer of 2008, Ogilvy was working on a new business presentation for Wachovia, then the fourth-largest US bank. It was our biggest pitch of the year. We had survived the initial rounds, and Wachovia had narrowed the selection down to us and one other firm. It was clear from the initial meeting that they were very interested in analytics (they were bankers, after all).

It was now time to present to Bob Steel, the CEO, and the Wachovia board. Usually we analytics folks get to tell our story at the beginning of the process, in the first few meetings, to show that our firm has the capabilities to tick the box, so to speak. The last meetings tend to be for the broad strategy and the creative. But since these bankers were so interested in the numbers, we decided to include analytics here as well.

The presentation went great. It was fun and interactive, and the bankers asked lots of questions. We went back to Manhattan happy and hopeful we would get the business. A few days later, shortly before noon, we got the call telling us we had. Later that day, I read an article online that Citibank might take over Wachovia, the first bank to go under in the financial crisis. We won the business, and it evaporated in a matter of hours.

After that, the entire world economy seemed to collapse for a while and we went into the great recession. During that period, it seemed everyone asked us how much they *needed* to spend on marketing. (Well, to be honest, they asked the question slightly differently. They said, "How much can I cut my marketing budget?")

So I looked at research on past recessions to see if there were any findings that would help us deal with this one. Reading through everything, I noticed very little new thinking. Most of the articles were either reruns of material that was written after past recessions or simply employed the same methodologies used in those articles to more recent data.

The most common approach was to compare the financial performance of companies that cut their advertising budgets during a recession to those who held their spending stable or even increased it. This methodology was first examined in the 1920s by Roland S. Vaile, and published in the *Harvard Business Review* in April 1927. Vaile compared companies that maintained their advertising spending during the 1923 recession to those that cut their budgets. He found that the biggest sales increases were recorded by companies that advertised the most. Vaile's research has been repeated during just about every recession ever since, and the results are always the same: Companies that cut their budgets during a recession performed worse during that recession and also in the subsequent years of recovery.

While the observations in all these studies are accurate, I often feel nervous about the recommendations derived from them. Most people claim the studies make a case for increasing investments during a recession in order to outmuscle weaker competitors and gain market share that can lead to a sustained advantage during the recovery and beyond. This implies causality, but none of the studies above delivers proof of this. Do companies that spend more during a recession perform better in the long run because they increased spending? Or are companies that perform well before, during, and after a recession better positioned to maintain or increase their spending during a recession? While some of the authors of these studies acknowledge these questions, none answered them.

I believe a more thorough approach is required to make the

case for sustained marketing investment during tough economic times, especially if we want the arguments to stand up to the scrutiny of already skeptical CFOs and CEOs. Three things can help here:

1. Increasing use of econometric modeling

2. Taking a holistic view of the marketing plan, i.e., a view that takes into account both media costs and media consumption habits during a recession

3. Determining the long-term effects of marketing and how they contribute to increased shareholder value

Let's deal with these points one at a time.

Increased use of econometric modeling. The most often quoted paper that uses econometric modeling to make a case for sustained investments throughout a recession is Paul Dyson's 2008 article "Cutting Adspend in Recession Delays Recovery" in a trade publication published by the World Advertising Research Center. The article uses econometric modeling to prove exactly what its title says. Specifically, Dyson showed that "the increased spend required during the recovery just to get back to pre-recession sales levels within a year will have to be around 60 per cent higher than the amount saved by cutting the ad budget in the first place." In other words, if I cut my ad budget by a dollar during the recession, I will need to spend an additional $1.60 to get back to even once it ends.

Taking a holistic view of the marketing plan. In determining whether (or by how much) to cut your marketing budget during a recession, you must take into account both media costs and media consumption. Costs are likely to fall during the recession, as radio and television stations, newspapers and magazines and Internet portals cut their prices to try to spur business.

There is also evidence that media consumption can change during a recession. People stay home and consume more media, which could increase the efficiency of media spending during tough times. Clearly an approach like this, which uses modeling and takes into account the specific context of the brand, the category, and the media landscape, is much more thorough and easier to defend than the one-size-fits-all "rules" described earlier.

Determining the long-term effects of marketing and how they contribute to increased shareholder value. Budget cuts during a recession are often the result of a short-term view. Advertising rarely pays for itself—let alone produces a profit—during the short run. Yet study after study shows that it increases shareholder value. (I know that sounds like a commercial for my industry, but I analyze data for a living, and the data shows it is true.) And research similar to Dyson's seems to show the converse is also true. Cutting ad budgets has an even greater (negative) effect over the long term. There is still a lot of work to be done to absolutely prove the case, and it should be done. The understanding of long-term effects of how much you spend on marketing is incredibly important, as it can impact shareholder value in the long term.

BUDGET ALLOCATION

Determining how much you should spend in good times and bad is only step one. Once you know the answer to "how much," then you need to ensure it is spent in the best way. So let's discuss how to align your budget to your marketing objectives, and allocate it across markets and across media.

I have seen companies get up to 30 percent more value out of their budget by getting these decisions right when they use the following framework.

Let's walk through the graphic below.

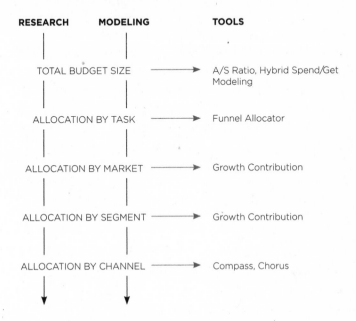

RESEARCH   MODELING   TOOLS

TOTAL BUDGET SIZE ——————————→ A/S Ratio, Hybrid Spend/Get Modeling

ALLOCATION BY TASK ——————————→ Funnel Allocator

ALLOCATION BY MARKET ——————————→ Growth Contribution

ALLOCATION BY SEGMENT ——————————→ Growth Contribution

ALLOCATION BY CHANNEL ——————————→ Compass, Chorus

We've already covered budget size. With allocation by task, you try to ensure that money is spent on what will give "the biggest bang for your buck." Many companies use the marketing funnel approach to drive customers to a purchasing decision by achieving these goals:

- *Awareness:* Making them know you exist

- *Consideration*: Making them think about you

- *Purchase:* Making them buy what you are selling

- *Loyalty:* Making them come back for more

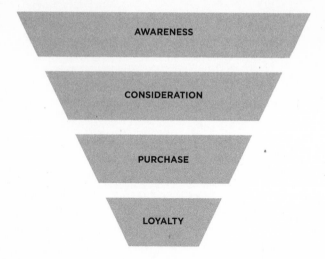

The levels of the funnel are the tasks needed to create demand. Each will have separate activities that cost money. The "Funnel Allocator" (a tool David Coppock developed) helps you decide how much to spend on each task.

The Funnel Allocator works on three stages:

1. Creating the revenue model

2. Creating the spend/get curves

3. Optimization

In creating the revenue model, you map out how sales are generated throughout the funnel. Let's say you are selling a new kind of Huggies diaper, and there are four million households that might buy it.

Some 80 percent are aware of your brand. That is 3.2 million households. Of those, 30 percent, or 960,000 households, would consider buying the diaper and, because of Huggies' strong reputation, some 50 percent of them actually do. That means you have 480,000 customers. We'll assume the average number of 64-packs they buy before their baby is toilet trained is 28.5. That means you have sold 1,824 diapers per baby. Figure the average price works out to be 20 cents a diaper, and it means $175 million in additional revenue.

Our funnel would look like this:

MARKET: 1 MILLION HOUSEHOLDS

AWARENESS — % Aware: 80%
Households considering: 3,200,000

CONSIDERATION — % Aware: 30%
Households considering: 960,000

PURCHASE — % Aware: 50%
Households considering: 480,000

LOYALTY — Average number of 64-pack diapers per customer: 28.5
Number of diapers sold: 1,825

Price product: $10
Revenue: 900,000

You can play around with this model and see, for example, that if you were to increase awareness from 80 percent to 81 percent, then revenues would increase by $2,190,000 (assuming performance at the other funnel levels stays the same).

Depending on how much it would cost to increase awareness from 80 percent to 81 percent, that may or may not be a good strategy. Maybe it is better to focus on purchase or loyalty. Again, that will depend on how much it would cost to move the needle for those tasks.

In stage two we create spend/get curves—usually using the hybrid approach for every level of the funnel. These spend/get curves would tell you *how much* awareness would increase by spending extra money trying to raise it.

The output of the second stage of the funnel allocator tool looks like this:

As you can see, you can get a spend/get curve for every funnel level.

The final stage is a simple optimization. Once you have created the spend/get curves, any fairly straightforward computer algorithm can use them to find the optimal spot on each curve, the place where you can maximize your marketing investment.

I first implemented this framework for a global technology company. They had asked me for help to determine how much they should spend on creating broad-based awareness of their company, and how much they should spend on converting that awareness and consideration into sales.

If you think about it, they were asking for a funnel with two layers: "Awareness and Consideration" at the top and "Demand Generation (DG)" at the bottom.

We had no econometric models available, nor did we have time to create any, so we built the curves using the hybrid method described on page 130. We ended up creating four different scenarios with different assumptions driving different shapes of the spend/get curves. Then we ran the optimization in each scenario to see how the proposed budget allocation changed as a result of changing the underlying assumptions. The figure below shows what we found:

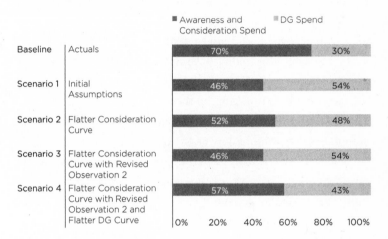

The results were very clear. At the starting point, 70 percent of their budget was spent on "Awareness and Consideration" activities and the rest on Demand Generation. All the scenarios we ran suggested that the split should probably be more in the area of 45 to 55 percent/55 to 45 percent.

The client really loved the analysis, for a number of reasons. First, there was nothing magical about it; everything was transparent. Second, it gave him an action plan: Reduce expenditures on awareness, and take that money and use it to increase demand generation spending. But what he loved most was that it helped him make assumptions about what would work and not work in a very systematic way.

This initial success with the approach got me excited. But subsequent conversations with other potential clients, people who were not comfortable with math, got me depressed.

Here's how one exchange went. I described the optimization process to a potential client, and she asked me how I had gotten the spend/get curves.

"We use whatever data is available and fill in the gaps with business judgment," I replied. "That's the beauty of this approach. It is really flexible and it incorporates data and common sense."

"We have no data," she said.

"No problem," I said, and I told her about my experience with the client who didn't have any data either but was still able to use the approach successfully.

"So you are just making up these curves?" she asked.

"If we have no data, we would make reasonable business assumptions that would allow us to do that, yes."

She immediately dismissed the approach and said she would never want to use such an unscientific approach for making multimillion-dollar decisions.

I asked her what she would use instead, in the absence of data.

She said they would go with one of the generic rules of thumb.

I was very disappointed. I knew I could help her, but I had not managed to convince her of the value of our approach. Instead, her company continued to make very ill-informed multimillion-dollar investment decisions. Specifically, they used the previous year's marketing budget as their baseline and adjusted it by how much corporate spending overall would increase in the following year. It is a very common approach; but, as we have seen, it is far from optimal.

This unsatisfying experience of dealing with a client who just couldn't see the value of analytics really helped me in the end. I learned that clients like the first one I worked with are rare. Most struggle to understand the value in simply making up these curves when the data is not available. It seems counterintuitive to them.

I figured out the reason for this. Because I had presented this way of determining how much to spend as a scientific tool with curves and optimization algorithms, I created the expectation that there must be a lot of data behind this. When there is, of course, you use the data. When there isn't, you make educated assumptions based on what you know. You have to make it up. And that phrase, "You have to make it up," can be unsettling.

So what I now do is talk about this approach as a decision-making tool that walks through a number of questions that need to be answered based on the data available and your business experience. What are those questions? They are the same ones asked in creating the spend/get curves:

- What is the current level of spending?
- What would our awareness be, if we didn't spend at all?
- What would awareness be if we had an unlimited budget?
- What do we think would happen if we altered our current spending (either up or down) by X percent?

The answer to those questions will suggest several investment allocation scenarios.

I got a lot less resistance when I positioned the tool that way. And today, if clients are still uncomfortable making assumptions, in the face of having no data—and some are—I tell them that no matter what other approach they take, they will still need to make assumptions anyway. They might just not be aware of doing it. For example, if you use advertising as a percent of sales to set your ad budget, you are assuming that your company is the same as other companies and has the same objectives—that one size fits all. That is a dangerous assumption to make.

The funnel allocation tool has become really successful. I think my explanation has helped. I also think that what accounts for the funnel allocation tool's increasing use is that it works. The approach of creating spend/get curves that are then used to run different optimization scenarios can be used just about any time you have to make an investment decision.

Let's discuss how to allocate your budget by country and by channel.

ALLOCATION BY COUNTRY

As we have seen, it's possible to make informed marketing investment decisions with very limited data or, even no data at all. All we need is time and a chance to collaborate with clients to create the spend/get curves. But sometimes you don't even have that! I am often asked to solve investment decision questions in a matter of days (or hours) with very little client collaboration. Even in these circumstances, you can use very basic math to make more informed investment decisions.

For example, I work with many global clients; at some point in the annual budgeting process, they need to decide how much marketing money should go to each country. (If your company isn't global, mentally substitute the various divisions/departments of your firm every time you read "country.") As you might imagine, this can be a highly political debate, with each country manager making their case for investment. Having a very transparent rationale for making country allocation decisions is therefore crucial.

The following simple approach can be implemented quickly. It is used by a number of global Fortune 100 companies, which have gotten a lot of benefit from it, simple though it is. It's so simple I almost didn't include it; but since clients seem to have benefited from the approach, here it is:

Step 1. Project the total revenue growth in the next year (or five years if you are looking at a longer horizon).

Step 2. Allocate the marketing dollars based on every country's share of that future revenue growth.

Step 3. Map every country on a two-by-two matrix based on their current revenue share—i.e., what percentage of the company's total sales they represent—and their future revenue growth. This gives you four quadrants, as shown in the diagram below:

REVENUE CONTRIBUTION TODAY

	Below Average	Above Average
Above Average (GROWTH TOMORROW)	**QUADRANT B** High Growth Low Current Contribution **AWARENESS-CENTRIC** Funnel Ratio - Top:bottom 70:30	**QUADRANT A** High Growth High Current Contribution **FULL 360** Funnel Ratio - Top:bottom 55:45
Below Average (GROWTH TOMORROW)	**QUADRANT D** Low Growth Low Current Contribution **DG HEAVY** Funnel Ratio - Top:bottom 10:90	**QUADRANT C** Low Growth High Current Contribution **DG CENTRIC** Funnel Ratio - Top:bottom 20:70

Let's break down what is in each quadrant.

- *Quadrant A* consists of countries with high current revenue and high revenue growth. They will get a lot of investment and their budgets should be spent across the entire marketing funnel.

- *Quadrant B* is made up of countries with low current revenue but projected high revenue growth. They should be spending most of their money at the top of the funnel to create brand awareness and consideration.

- In *Quadrant C* are those countries with high current revenue but low projected revenue growth. They will be well established and therefore will need to spend less at the top of the funnel and more on activities that try and convert the established presence into sales.

- *Quadrant D* is countries with low current revenue and low revenue growth. Obviously, this is the place to invest the least, and what money is spent here should go toward driving sales.

A more sophisticated approach would be to create spend/get curves for every country, if you can, based on actual data. However, if you do not have the data or the time to get it, this simple framework can be very useful in determining where you should put your resources. It can also be helpful in explaining why you might be cutting someone's budget; it's so simple, it's hard to argue with.

ALLOCATION BY MEDIUM

The last allocation question deals with media. The media mix used by companies today can be very complex because there are so many options to choose from—everything from the traditional (radio, TV, and print) to search, online banners, social networks, in-store displays, mobile, email, SMS, RSS feeds, blogs, iPhone apps—the list goes on and on and seems to grow every day. Knowing what proportion of your budget to spend on each medium has therefore become a complicated task. It's so complicated that an entire industry of media mix modeling providers has popped up, companies such as Marketshare Partners, Hudson River Group, Milward Brown Optimor, Analytic

Partners, M-Factor, MMA, to name just a few. They all use data and advanced statistical algorithms to answer the complex question: What media should we use to reach our customers and potential customers? To answer that question, ultimately they will all look to create the spend/get curves we have been talking about. They will create a curve for every medium that allows them to build optimization scenarios that allocate the budget by medium.

At the very basic level, there are two ways they can do this: they can use historical data or survey data. We will cover a third option—individual level attribute modeling—in Chapter 6.

Historical data is exactly what it sounds like. You look back at how your media mix has changed over time and you examine those changes to see how they affected business results. You can use the econometric modeling techniques we discussed earlier in this chapter. The advantage here is that you are dealing with real numbers—basing your decision on real historical facts. Unfortunately, that's also the main limitation with the approach. If you are doing something radically new, then the past will be less relevant in predicting what the future will look like. For example, if you have used only TV, radio, and print previously, then the past won't tell you much about how much to spend on search in the future. Similarly, if you are going to spend only half of what you did in the past, your historical patterns again will probably fail to predict the future.

This is why historical analysis is often complemented with additional research. There are a number of vendors that collect data on how customers consume media and how that impacts their purchasing decisions. This data can then be used to construct the spend/get curves for every medium. The Dutch company Pointlogic collects this kind of data. It allows companies to create spend/get curves for all sorts of marketing tasks, as the graphic below shows.

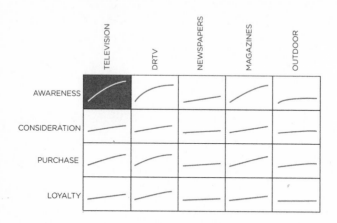

The advantage of adding research is that it gives you data on channels you might never have used before. The downside is that it can be pretty expensive to gather that data yourself.

You can certainly find partners to help you with media mix modeling. If you go out looking, you might want to take along the following list to make sure you are getting exactly the help that you need.

How to Choose Your Partner

Whether you are using historical data or surveys or some combination, here are the key things you will need to do in order to optimize your marketing investment:

1. *Gather data* on marketing spending and performance from a wide range of sources.

2. *Aggregate that data.* Put all the data in one place where it can be accessed easily by the people who will be doing the analysis.

3. *Statistical modeling.* Build statistical models that link marketing spend to business outcomes.

4. *Optimization.* Use those statistical models to determine what is the optimal marketing spend and allocation.

5. *Scenario planning.* To determine all your options, build several investment scenarios that demonstrate the impact of different investment strategies on business performance.

6. *Dashboards and management systems.* You want to give nontechnical users access to the data and scenarios through a decision support system that makes it easy for them to understand what you have found. Building dashboards, as we will discuss in Chapter 6, is one simple way to do it.

7. *Strategic consulting and planning.* You need to help decision makers to make the most of all of the above and guide them on how they can use these tools for decision making. These tasks map perfectly to the market differentiators that started to emerge throughout my conversations with the various vendors, as you can see from the following graphic:

REQUIRED CAPABILITIES	MARKET DIFFERENTIATORS
DATA GATHERING	DATA ACCESS
DATA AGGREGATION	AUTOMATED DATA PREPARATION
STATISTICAL MODELING	UNIQUE ALGORITHMS
OPTIMIZATION	DECISION SUPPORT TOOLS
SCENARIO PLANNING	DECISION SUPPORT TOOLS
OPTIMIZATION	DECISION SUPPORT TOOLS
STRATEGIC CONSULTING AND PLANNING	ADDED VALUE SERVICES

Let me tell you what I found in a bit more detail.

Data access. Some vendors have access to special data sources through alliances they have with third-party data vendors or search engines.

Automated data preparation. Data preparation can use up a lot of your resources, no matter what you plan to do with your sexy little numbers on projects like these. You have to figure out what to ask, ask it, total the results, check the totals, put the results into buckets, do the analysis—you get the idea. It's a lot of work. Some vendors have automated several of these steps so they can do the data gathering and aggregation described above faster, better, and more cost-effectively than you can.

Unique algorithms. The algorithms have been around for decades, so you might think all econometric modeling skills are pretty level. However, you would be surprised how much variance there is in the quality of the statistical modeling between different vendors. Make sure you look underneath the hood and ask who is actually doing the modeling. (Is it someone who has been doing this work for a while, or are you signing up with a firm that will have low-level people actually do the work.)

Decision support tools. Some vendors offer dashboards and scenario planning and decision support tools. These tools can be extremely useful for helping the end users—especially those without a mathematics/scientific background—adopt some of the scientific evidence into their decision making.

Value added services. This is probably the most important area. I have seen so many modeling projects collect dust on the shelf of the marketing intelligence managers. Building models is easy. Using them always seems to be difficult. Look for a partner who can help you with both.

Whether you will work with a vendor in this space or do it yourself, make sure you have all the resources you need—and none that you don't (because who wants to waste money?).

GETTING IT RIGHT

A lot of good things can happen when you make the right budgeting decisions. In Chapter 7 we will discuss how TD Ameritrade used science to optimize all their digital marketing efforts. Here we will show how they used some of the techniques described earlier to change their media mix drastically over time as well.

During the dot-com bubble, TDA had a lot of their media dollars stuck in expensive broad-based channels such as national TV. After the bubble burst, and trading volume dropped dramatically, they could no longer afford those expensive channels. So we worked with them to reshuffle their media mix. Specifically, we looked at two of the decisions described in this chapter: how much to spend by task and how much to spend by medium.

For the task allocation, we used the funnel allocator. TDA had a relatively straightforward funnel, as shown in the figure below.

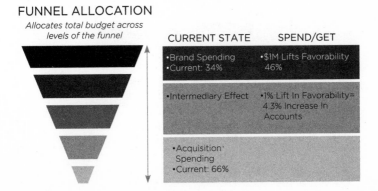

FUNNEL ALLOCATION

Allocates total budget across levels of the funnel

	CURRENT STATE	SPEND/GET
	•Brand Spending •Current: 34%	•$1M Lifts Favorability 46%
	•Intermediary Effect	•1% Lift In Favorability= 4.3% Increase In Accounts
	•Acquisition Spending •Current: 66%	

We decided to look at two levels: brand spending that would create awareness ("Yes, I have heard of TD Ameritrade") and favorability ("I like the company"), as well as acquisition spending that would help convert that favorability to getting people actually to sign up and trade with the company. We found through research that a 1 percent lift in favorability would increase the number of accounts that were opened by 4.3 percent. This demonstrated the link between performance at the top of the funnel and performance at the bottom.

We then created spend/get curves for the two funnel levels and ran optimization scenarios. These scenarios confirmed that TDA was currently spending the right proportion of their budget on both funnel levels.

In the second stage, we moved on to the media allocation. We used a combination of outside vendor Pointlogic's research and econometric modeling to shift the media budget.

As a result of the research, we saw what had to change. And so:

- Print budgets more than doubled.
- TV budgets were reduced 20 percent.
- Banner ad budgets were cut 19 percent.
- The money eliminated from the banner ad budget was shifted into streaming video.

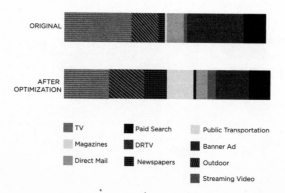

Because we did the allocation in this two-step process, we were able to create a media mix for every funnel level. This is shown in the graph below.

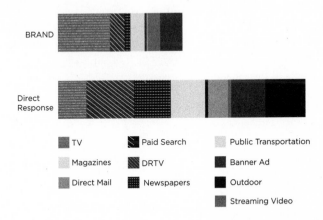

As a result of this exercise, we were able to shift a significant amount of the expensive TV dollars into cheaper direct-response TV (infomercials) and digital media, saving the company millions, while still achieving their financial objectives.

THINGS TO DO MONDAY MORNING

1. *Put these tools to work.* Unfortunately, for most companies, the major take-away from this chapter is a negative. The reality is that far too few marketers are using econometric modeling to really understand the impact of their marketing efforts on their business. Don't be one of them. Don't be one of those marketers who end up making multimillion-dollar decisions on pure gut feel. Whether the overall economy is good or bad, that will ultimately get you into trouble!

2. *Start by trying out Harry Henry's basic rules of thumb.* Yes, they are very crude measures, but you can calculate them quickly and that will give you an initial idea of where you are, and

you can use those figures as a starting point to figure out different spend levels.

3. *Use our guide to start the conversation* with specialist companies who can help you optimize your marketing budget.

4. *Finally, sit down with your three most important marketing goals in front of you.* Determine which of the tools we talked about will help make them a reality.

CHAPTER SIX

YARDSTICKS: HOW DO YOU MEASURE WHAT WORKS AND WHAT DOESN'T?

Not only can you target who you believe are the right customers, but you now also have the tools to build a plan for reaching them using the right tactics, media, and budget.

But once you create and implement that plan, how can you know which components are working and which are not? Sure, you can get an overall picture—sales went up 12 percent or earnings dropped 4 percent—but that is in the aggregate. Remember, our objective is to measure how effective each dollar spent is toward reaching our goals. One overall measure doesn't do that.

Thanks to a recent explosion in metrics, everything is now measurable (and we will touch on all your options within this chapter). But here's the big take-away in what you are about to read. The measurements need to be friendly. People are overwhelmed by all the numbers available. That's why you need to create measurements that are both easily understood and quickly grasped. In the pages ahead, I will show you:

1. What to measure
2. How to measure it (and how to find what you need to measure)
3. How to display what you have so it is easily understood by everyone
4. A case study that will show how all this plays out in practice

I've always been a geek. I got my first computer when I was nine. It was a ZX Spectrum with 16K in memory. That means all it could hold was a few sentences of text.

A few of my friends and I started taking BASIC computer programming classes when we were ten. We thought we were normal kids, but in retrospect, it was very geeky. I mean, what "average" ten-year-olds are into programming? Still, I was soon able to create my first computer game (which was also my last). It involved a little blue Pac-Man–like thing that ate green cactuses on a yellow screen.

When the Internet came along, I was an early adopter as well. I remember the day the first PCs with Internet access were installed in the computer room of the University of Antwerp. A small group of enthusiasts (geeks again, I am afraid) soon started to spend hours in that room. We were there when they opened at eight in the morning and we closed it at nine in the evening. (Surfing the web took time in those days. Very basic images took a couple of minutes to load.)

This same curiosity carried forward into my early professional life. When marketers began using the Internet for communications purposes, it soon became apparent that enormous amounts of data were being gathered on the servers that hosted those web pages. The promise for analytics was huge. Everything was measurable. I could track every click and every interaction people had with our clients' websites.

I did a project for one of our clients in Belgium just after the launch of one of their first websites. I called up the Belgian Internet service provider and asked them if they could send me the server log files, the place where they record and keep all the activity on any website they host, our client's in this case.

"What would you need those for?" the person on the other end of the line asked.

I explained I wanted to trawl through them to figure out how our client's customers were using the new website.

"Interesting idea," he said. (That was in 1997. Recently, Forrester Research predicted that web analytics in the United States alone will be a $1 billion industry by 2014!)

The log looked something like this:

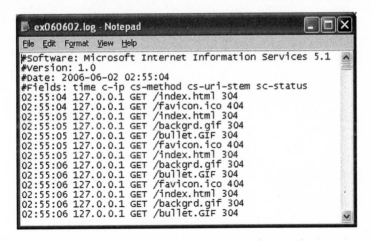

```
📄 ex060602.log - Notepad                        _ □ ✕

File  Edit  Format  View  Help
#Software: Microsoft Internet Information Services 5.1
#Version: 1.0
#Date: 2006-06-02 02:55:04
#Fields: time c-ip cs-method cs-uri-stem sc-status
02:55:04 127.0.0.1 GET /index.html 304
02:55:04 127.0.0.1 GET /favicon.ico 404
02:55:05 127.0.0.1 GET /index.html 304
02:55:05 127.0.0.1 GET /backgrd.gif 304
02:55:05 127.0.0.1 GET /bullet.GIF 304
02:55:05 127.0.0.1 GET /favicon.ico 404
02:55:05 127.0.0.1 GET /index.html 304
02:55:06 127.0.0.1 GET /backgrd.gif 304
02:55:06 127.0.0.1 GET /bullet.GIF 304
02:55:06 127.0.0.1 GET /favicon.ico 404
02:55:06 127.0.0.1 GET /index.html 304
02:55:06 127.0.0.1 GET /backgrd.gif 304
02:55:06 127.0.0.1 GET /bullet.GIF 304
```

Now don't get scared. It's just data. Raw data. If you look closely at this log, you'll see there are a number of constants.

> *Time.* This snapshot was taken at 2:55 (and four seconds) in the morning.
>
> *IP address.* As we explained earlier, this can be thought of as the phone number of the computer that is browsing. In this case the "phone number" was 127.0.0.1
>
> *GET.* This means there was a request to obtain an asset.
>
> *Sc-status.* This is a code that shows whether the GET command was successful (304 means it was).

From the first row, we can see that at 2:55 a.m. computer number 127.0.0.1 asked the server to show the client's home page, and the request was fulfilled successfully. In the subsequent rows, you can see that the same computer asked for a whole bunch of other assets at almost exactly the same time. Most of these are pictures on the home page. (The server log will record all these requests separately.) The files I got about activity on our client's site had millions of these rows. I started to combine them to see what individuals did when they visited the website.

I am explaining all this for two reasons: first, to demonstrate that there is nothing magical or overly complex about data; if you spend a bit of time with it, you will see that it's all very logical. Second, it illustrates how, especially on the web, everything is measurable.

At the time I was messing around with these server log files there were a bunch of smarter kids in Silicon Valley who saw the potential of this and started to develop software packages—Webtrends Log Analyzer was probably the most popular in the early days of web analytics—that would do all the compilation work for you. They would go through all these server log files, and then spit out a seventy-page report every day with hundreds of metrics on what was happening on your website. What took me days of hard work was now available in a single mouse click. Once I got access to Webtrends, I set up automatic feeds for all of my clients. Every morning they would open their mailboxes and find a seventy-page report on all the activity on their websites from the previous day. There was a lot of excitement in the beginning. "All that data—unbelievable." "Everything is measurable!" "This is incredibly powerful."

However, the honeymoon period was short and it was followed by a long period of silence. My clients really struggled with the data. There were too many metrics to digest. It soon became apparent that seventy pages every day was overkill. But even when we went to weekly and then biweekly reports, we found very little interest. When I asked why, my clients said, "There is no context. What does it mean if I have five thousand visits to my site a day or that my visitors spend two minutes and fifty-two seconds on average on my home page? Is that good or bad?"

This was the real problem. We had been too focused on what we *could* measure, not enough on what we *should* measure.

We got carried away by the technology—and measured everything, instead of focusing on the metrics that mattered.

MEASURE WHAT MATTERS

While I was struggling with this, I found someone in our London office, Adrian Jarvis, who was facing exactly the same problem. I remember giving him a call and barely being able to understand him. Adrian was from a little town called Hull in northern England and I had never heard a northern English accent before. But I got the hang of it quickly, and we started to crack our problem—how could we help our clients make sense of all this data the web was gathering?—together.

We soon decided our main mistake had been skipping the measurement planning stage. We hadn't spent enough time thinking about what we needed to measure. What were the few data points that were really going to help our clients determine whether what they were doing online was successful?

To find out, the very first question we needed to ask our clients was, "What is success?" Adrian and I discovered that when we started our measurement projects with our clients with a conversation around what they were trying to achieve, everything that followed made a lot more sense.

To make those conversations go even more smoothly, we borrowed from work that had been done in other fields. Management consultants have been advising clients for decades on how to formulate their strategies by defining what success meant. For example, *The Balanced Scorecard: Translating Strategy into Action*, by Robert S. Kaplan and David P. Norton, showed managers how to assess the cause and effect of different critical factors on strategic success. Specifically, they suggested leaders concentrate on four critical areas:

- *Financial.* How are we perceived by our shareholders?
- *Customers.* How are we perceived by our customers?
- *Process perspective.* In what processes should we excel in order to succeed?
- *Learning and Innovation.* How will we sustain our ability to change and improve?

We liked Kaplan and Norton's thinking, but we wanted something more tailored to marketing in general and Internet marketing in particular. We also wanted a process we could walk through with clients, as well as a framework for implementing measurement systems. What we eventually came up with became known as OgilvyEvaluate, and it has become the standard measurement approach for our global advertising and marketing network. While it started as a tool for web management, it soon became clear that it could be used for any type of measurement.

I still use the framework today. A lot of the measurement technology has changed in the last couple of years but the Evaluate approach hasn't. That's because it is basic common sense. And common sense is timeless.

Shortly after Adrian and I developed the framework, a huge ($35 billion in revenue) electronics company wanted to put together a global multichannel marketing campaign. This was the ideal opportunity to implement Evaluate. We explained the approach to the client, they liked it, and we set a date for the first deliverable, which is the Evaluate workshop.

The workshop is the most powerful and straightforward part of the process. The idea is to get the key decision makers in one room and, through a four-step process, have them agree on key performance indicators (KPIs; i.e., success metrics) and specifics about how the numbers will be measured and reported. Let me show you the steps.

Prioritizing of objectives. This is the most fundamental part of the entire process and the one companies most often skip when putting in place a measurement system. And that's a real shame because when you get this wrong, everything else you do from a measurement point of view will not be effective.

To get it right, participants first define what success will look like by writing the objectives of the program they want to develop.

No two people from the electronics company had the same list. In fact, the lists were wildly different. The head of manufacturing thought it was all about moving product. The woman in charge of marketing believed it was all about learning more about their customers, so they could sell other parts of their line; and the finance guy was interested only in the short-term ROI. This was very surprising, since almost all the people in the room were the marketing executives who had been planning this campaign together for months. But this experience was definitely not an anomaly. In the years since, I've run into it again and again. If you don't make the objectives crystal clear, then people will very quickly develop their own thoughts about what success means. The consequences can be incredibly counterproductive.

In the case of the electronics company, we had a healthy discussion about what success meant and at the end of the exercise came to a very clear articulation everyone agreed with. The exercise took much longer than I had anticipated, so my tight schedule for the workshop was out the window; but that didn't matter. We had just had a discussion that not only helped the measurement plan; it also helped focus the strategy of the entire campaign.

Rewriting objectives. Rewriting the objective is a simple, but incredibly useful, exercise. Objectives are only real objectives if they have a metric, a benchmark, and a time frame.

If they don't have each of these three components, they are more loose aims or aspirations. So, during this step in the process, we go through the list of objectives from the previous exercise and reformulate them to make sure they contain all three components.

At Ogilvy, for example, our mission is "to be most valued by those who value brands." That in and of itself is not an objective. To make it so, we might say "to achieve our goal we will" (and here I am making up the numbers):

- Increase revenue per employee by 22 percent annually
- Increase the number of employees who can use our knowledge management system from 65 percent to 80 percent within two years
- Reduce forecasting errors from 20 percent to 5 percent by Q3

Each of our additions has a metric, a target, and a time frame. This approach is similar to "SMART objectives," which you may have heard of in the context of discussing the best way to achieve a goal. A smart objective is:

- **Specific.** Objectives should clearly specify what they want to achieve.
- **Measurable.** You should be able to track whether you are meeting the objectives or not.
- **Achievable.** Stretch goals are encouraged.
- **Realistic.** Can you really achieve the objectives with the resources you have?
- **Time based.** When do you want to achieve the set objectives?

By reformulating your objectives to make sure they are SMART, you automatically create a list of your most important Key Performance Indicators. This list is the starting point of the next exercise. But before we discuss the KPIs, we need to spend a moment on how we are going to judge how well they are doing. And to do that, we need to talk, briefly, about benchmarking.

Benchmarking is about context. You can choose the right metric. But when you get the numbers back, how do you know if they are good or bad? That's the question benchmarking is designed to answer. By comparing your company to others that are doing the same thing, you have a way of rating your performance.

There are two ways to obtain benchmark information: from external sources and by developing your own internal data. And there are all kinds of applications and products to help you there. (We will be talking about specific tools later in the chapter.)

But you may not have to do a lot of research to judge your performance. Often the best benchmark is a comparison versus your own performance over time. Yes, it is a very common measure, but you would be amazed how often marketers forget to use it. At Ogilvy we are trying not to be guilty of that. Our analytics team has started to capture results from campaigns we run all around the world. We put them into a common database that can be queried for benchmarks. So, for example, if you are running a direct mail campaign for a financial institution in the United States, you can look at what kinds of returns those campaigns typically generate, and compare your performance to theirs.

Action learning indicators. Putting in place and measuring the right key performance indicators that enable you to focus on achieving success is often not enough. You need to know why a certain metric goes up or down. Action learning indicators come into play by providing insights into what drives certain KPIs.

For the electronics company, one KPI was the number of

new customers acquired through a marketing campaign. This KPI had a whole range of action learning indicators associated with it—acquisitions by product, segment, geography. . . .

It is important here to have a broad range of metrics that will not only enable you to assess the performance of your campaigns but also let you understand why you are performing as you are.

Data source mapping + measurement plan. Once the list of KPIs and action learning indicators is complete, we can move on to mapping metrics to data sources and actually begin the tracking to see how well we are doing.

A typical multichannel measurement system will use data from a broad range of sources (we will cover some of them later in the chapter). Some companies have these sources integrated into an all-encompassing corporate data warehouse. But most don't. They are spread out all over the place. The implementation stage usually involves a lot of data integration.

Once we know how to find the data we need, we start measuring performance.

What Should You Be Measuring?

The most basic element of the measurement plan is understanding exactly what you are going to measure. You need to look at three types of metrics.

Inputs. What are we investing to grow demand? Let's go back to our Huggies example. Say I want to acquire new customers in order to grow demand. To do that, I might run a few print ads in the baby and new parents magazines and spend some money buying baby-related search terms on Google. The inputs could be the money spent on print and search.

Outputs. What are the results generated from these investments? The output could be the print and search impressions we get for that investment as well as the awareness and likability of the print ads and the clicks and click-through rate for my search advertising.

Outcomes. How is what we ultimately want to achieve impacted by what we invest in any incremental new customers that are acquired? Let's look at these three categories of metrics in more detail.

Input metrics measure the resources you put into your efforts at growing demand. Surprisingly, this cost data is often hard to get to. It tends to be stored in finance systems in a way that is not always useful for analysis. It's usually pretty easy to get total spend, but it is often impossible to look at spend by the main activities you are putting in place to impact your business.

Let's say that at the end of the evaluation process, I understood that creating brand awareness and increasing product trial among young men were my two main objectives. I'd put in place marketing programs in order to achieve these goals and then I would try to track performance of these programs against my two main objectives.

I say "try" because most companies I have worked with would not be able to look at the marketing costs split by these two objectives. That's because corporate finance systems are often built by people who do not really care about tracking the costs aligned to marketing goals. They just don't get that granular. Companies that have identified this problem, and put in place the often very easy fixes, tend to increase dramatically their ability to track ROI of all the different activities.

Useful investment metrics for inputs are spending by marketing objective, geography, medium, customer segment, and marketing program.

After we implemented a measurement framework for a Fortune 50 B2B company, the chief marketing officer told us she finally had a very granular understanding of how they were spending their marketing dollars. She now knew exactly where the money was going (before they had not done any breakdown beyond broad categories such as "print" or "online") and what the results were by channel, campaign and country. This may sound very basic, but in my experience this client is one of the very few companies that really understands this. Most organizations I have worked with know how much they spend and how they allocate it by region and business unit, but that's where it usually ends. Not surprisingly, as a result of what she learned, our client shifted money away from things that were not working well—traditional print—to things that were: ads on the business and Sunday morning television shows and targeted email and direct mail.

Output metrics track the immediate impact of your activities by measuring the engagement people have with your campaign. Engagement is important in measurement because, in the digital world, marketers can easily see how consumers interact with the messages they put out into the marketplace.

A simple example comparing TV to online video will show you what engagement is all about. For traditional television, it is possible only to measure the amount of TV advertising you are putting in the market (measured by TV "impressions"), how many people remember the spot, and if they liked it.

For online video, you can measure that, plus:

- The exact number of viewers and the number of times each one watched the video

- Whether they watched the video all the way through, fast-forwarded sections, sent it to friends, embedded it in a site, or wrote a comment about it

- We could even analyze the comments and measure the number of people who were positive about it versus negative.

You clearly see that people can interact (or engage) with digital content in many more different ways, all of them measurable. This increased visibility regarding how people engage with content can go a long way in helping improve it.

Here is a framework to help measure engagement.

DIMENSION	EXAMPLE GENERIC DIGITAL METRICS	
EXPOSURE	Display media impressions/ reach, organic searches, video viewings, page views/ visits, podcasts/ vidcasts/blog (RSS) subscriptions	DECREASING AUDIENCE SIZE
RESPONSE	Banner click, organic search referrals, percentage viewed, completed videos, geo-response (e.g., number of countries responding)	
INTERACTION	Downloads, new subscriptions, website actions completed	
PARTICIPATION	Forum members, votes cast, survey response, blog comments, conversation depth	
DISCUSSION	Opinions, external blog comments, trackbacks, wiki participation	INCREASING AUDIENCE VALUE
ADVOCACY	Number of blogs discussing topic, rich media response (e.g., video response), percent of active members	

The farther you move down the table, the deeper the engagement and the higher the value of the consumers who are at that level. Ultimately, of course, you are trying to reach "advocacy." Today it is very easy for people to share their opinion on blogs and social networks. This makes advocacy (positive or negative) even more important.

Outcome variables measure whether you are achieving your goals, i.e., whether you are beating the targets you set. Intermediate metrics show whether our marketing objectives are being achieved through measures such as:

- *Brand awareness*: How many people know about our brand, product, or service?

- *Brand favorability:* How many people like the brand, product, or service?

- *Brand consideration:* How many people would think about buying it?

- *Acquisition:* How many new customers have we attracted?

- *Loyalty:* How many customers are loyal to the brand? Each company has to determine what loyalty means for them. It could be frequency of purchase; the fact that they bought within the last thirty days; share of wallet; length of the relationship or, as is usually the case, some combination of the above.

While these metrics tell you how well you are achieving your marketing objectives, they don't necessarily show the impact on the business. This is where business metrics come into play. These include:

> Market share
>
> Revenue
>
> Profit
>
> Average basket size (how much customers are buying from you in any given transaction)
>
> ROI
>
> Share price

These are the metrics that assess the impact of your efforts on overall business health. The key here is to isolate the impact of what you are doing on the fluctuations in these metrics. You want to filter out all other factors that can affect results so that you can concentrate on one variable at a time. This gets to the attribution question, which we will talk about later in this chapter.

Putting in Place the Tracking Mechanisms

Once you decide what you want to measure, you can go and find the data. Here is a very quick overview of some of the most common data sources you will be able to use for measuring your success.

Corporate finance systems. These can give you the ultimate outcome metrics such as sales and profit. They usually can provide the numbers by geography, business unit, customer segment, and other dimensions. Finance systems often also give you benchmarks and forecasts for the key business metrics. This data provides context for interpreting the business metrics. Did you hit your target; did you beat the forecast; etc. Metrics without context are useless.

Media and marketing plans. If finance systems can provide context for the main business metrics, marketing and media plans do the same for the more intermediate marketing and media metrics that we talked about earlier.

Transactional databases. We discussed in Chapter 2 how to identify people we want to communicate with. These databases often get aggregated into the corporate finance systems that provide data on the overall performance of an organization. However, sometimes it is important to get the more granular behavioral data, for example, if you are interested in tracking the performance of a particular customer segment.

Customer relationship management systems. CRM systems often store tons of data about direct interactions with customers. They tend to track who you targeted; what you targeted them with; and what the response and follow-up were. If your company has a sales force, then the sales force systems—which track your salespeople's interactions with your customers or prospects—can be a great complement to the CRM systems.

Market research. While we discussed market research in the context of getting the insights that can help you determine what to communicate to your targets (Chapter 3), market research is often also a crucial data source for measurement of your performance, especially for intermediate metrics such as awareness, favorability, familiarity with the brand, etc. These types of metrics are not captured in corporate finance systems or transactional databases. You don't tell the cashier at the checkout that you bought a bar of Dove soap because you love the campaign for "real beauty" and you feel it reflects your core values. The only way to track how people are feeling about a brand is by asking a sample of consumers through market research. Surprisingly, the costs and time involved in tracking surveys are much smaller than you might think. Market research no longer needs to be expensive and time-consuming. Companies such as Dynamic Logic have made research fast and affordable online by allowing you to target research respondents much more precisely. Your questionnaire can be triggered by specific actions.

Let's say you sell lawn mowers for a living and you have questions about features your potential customers are looking for. Typically, you would send out a questionnaire but, despite your best efforts—you did a mailing only to the suburbs, for example—a lot of your marketing expense will be wasted. There are apartment buildings and condos in the suburbs, and the people who live there don't buy lawn mowers. But you can have your survey pop up when someone visits the lawn mower page at Wal-Mart (providing, of course, you have permission). Odds are, that person is very interested in mowers. And you get even more specific. Suppose you are targeting lawn mower buyers who are safety-conscious because they have small children. It is possible to have your survey pop up only after someone has viewed both mowers and children's toys on the web.

In addition to these more traditional data sources we have just talked about, there is a wide range of other resources you can draw on for incredible amounts of data you can use to assess the performance of a campaign.

Web analytics. An entire industry has developed recently comprised of companies that specialize in capturing and analyzing the tons of data generated by websites. What's great is that they have automated many of the data manipulation tasks that need to be done to produce analysis. This means that everyone can learn how to use these tools easily. And it doesn't have to cost a lot. Indeed, it can be free.

Google Analytics, for example, is a free web analytics software package that does an excellent job of capturing and explaining a company's web data. It is extremely easy to install and even easier to use. Once installed, it will automatically start to track your website activity. You can access the statistics online through a very user friendly interface. You can even set up email alerts that let you know when your traffic has spiked. And again, it is free. I am a fan. You can learn more at http://www.google.com/analytics/. Yahoo! has a similar service (http://web.analytics.yahoo.com/). Other web analytics vendors such as Omniture and Webtrends provide more advanced web analytics solutions but charge a fee.

Social network data. Knowing what customers and prospects do on your website is no longer enough. An increasing number of interactions are happening outside of your website on social networks and in the blogosphere. We have already discussed (see Chapter 4) how some software packages analyze what people are writing on the web and how this can give you an idea of how consumers talk about your brand and what they talk about. These software packages can also be used to track the volume of conversations online about your brand and they can also quantify the sentiment of those conversations.

Interactions on social platforms such as Facebook and Myspace can also be monitored. Facebook has a service, Facebook Insight, that will show you how many fans your page has, how many visitors, etc. Facebook is also proving to be a really powerful market research and tracking tool. Millions of people are expressing their opinions about everything every day. Facebook's analytics team uses that tremendous wealth of data to uncover trends about brands—including products and politicians. For example, a graph about the "Obama brand" tracks the president's approval ratings, and the results are almost identical to the numbers produced by traditional pollsters such as Gallup and Rasmussen. That's pretty impressive. In addition, Facebook is now able to give brands real-time access to tracking information. I have seen them run polls in real time that generated over a thousand responses in less than two minutes. It could take a traditional polling organization weeks, if not months, to generate these kinds of results. Facebook produces the same results in a fraction of the time and with far less cost.

Digital ad serving platforms. Online advertising and search are accounting for an increasingly large proportion of most companies' spends on marketing. These channels also generate enormous amounts of data that can be used for measurement. The companies that serve up the banner ads have reporting interfaces that can let you know how many banners were presented, where they were served, at what cost, and how many people clicked through.

Online videos. These are playing an increasingly big part in the media mix of most companies, and YouTube is by far the largest video platform. It involves a reporting tool that provides statistics about how many people have interacted with your videos. You want to know how you are being perceived. There are so many things you can measure that it is easy to see how you could get lost in the data. And even if you know what you want to measure, you need to make it easy for the people who will use the data to get access to it. This is where marketing dashboards can be of incredible help. They pull together the pieces of information you need to run your business and display them in one view. For example, Ogilvy Live collates data from the various reporting tools described above and automatically presents it in a single view.

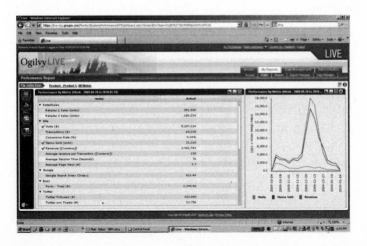

VISUALIZATION OF DATA

There is so much data available that data visualization has become a separate specialist field at the intersection of art and science. Data visualization shows how to display information in a way that makes it easy to understand. Its godfather is Edward Tufte.

Tufte's 1983 book, *The Visual Display of Quantitative Information*, is the most important book ever written on the subject. It is packed with examples of best and worst practices in the history of data visualization. The book itself is beautiful. Tufte wanted its design to follow his principles, so he decided to publish it himself, having to take a second mortgage to finance it. I warn you, once you read Tufte, you will become allergic to graphs that break his rules.

For our purposes I just want to touch on three of those rules here. I urge you to read Tufte's entire book (once you are done with mine).

Rule 1. Graphical Integrity. Tufte believes, and I agree, that visual representations of data must tell the truth. (Don't make small numbers look graphically big.) Here's an example of what not to do.

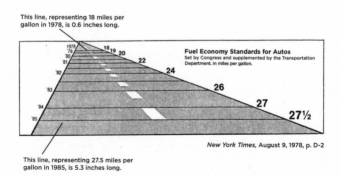

This line, representing 18 miles per gallon in 1978, is 0.6 inches long.

Fuel Economy Standards for Autos
Set by Congress and supplemented by the Transportation Department. In miles per gallon.

New York Times, August 9, 1978, p. D-2

This line, representing 27.5 miles per gallon in 1985, is 5.3 inches long.

Rule 2. Data-Ink is the ink of the graph that represents data. Tufte believes good graphical representations maximize data-ink and eliminate as much non-data-ink as possible. An electroencephalogram would be the classic good example.

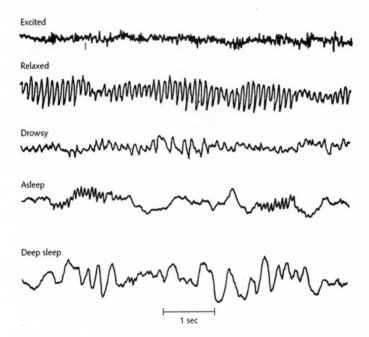

Excited

Relaxed

Drowsy

Asleep

Deep sleep

1 sec

You can tell at a glance what is going on, and there is nothing superfluous about the representations.

Rule 3. Keep it simple. Draw attention to the data. Or, "no chart junk." Tufte devotes an entire chapter to what he calls chart junk—the excessive and unnecessary use of graphical effects where the designer draws attention to himself instead of the data. Here is what he calls possibly the worst graph ever, which appeared in an education magazine in the 1970s.

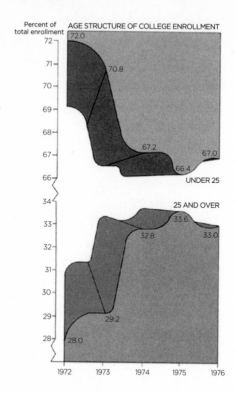

Percent of total enrollment — AGE STRUCTURE OF COLLEGE ENROLLMENT

Thanks in part to Tufte, I have become allergic to chart junk.

CAUSE AND EFFECT

By implementing the measurement principles we have discussed, you can develop a set of performance indicators for tracking performance over time to see how you are doing. But that is only part of measurement. Knowing how well you are doing is one thing, finding out how what you are doing affects (or doesn't affect) your performance is another.

To use a simple example, when Toyota sales slumped a couple of years ago, it wasn't because its advertising suddenly became ineffective. It was because misaligned floor mats were getting in the way of the gas pedal, causing accidents and scaring off potential buyers. That brings us to attribution. If I am measuring the impact of a marketing campaign on sales, then I need not only to track sales but also specifically to learn how the campaign impacts sales. In other words, what portion of the incremental increase in sales is being caused by my actions? The two approaches for measuring attribution are econometric modeling and individual level attribution.

Econometric modeling, as discussed in Chapter 5, uses mathematics to estimate the laws of supply and demand. It helps determine to what extent demand for a product is driven by price, the income of consumers, and other attributes, such as your marketing and promotional efforts.

My colleagues in China used econometric modeling to demonstrate the impact of their advertising efforts on Motorola's sales. Motorola's brand image in China in the mid-1990s was weak. Qualitative research found that Motorola was perceived as suitable "for older businessmen, but not for me." Even Motorola users thought Motorola phones lacked style.

This was a big problem in China. How a cell phone looks really matters. A phone is something you wear. Chinese consumers said in research that the brand was the most important factor in their choice of phone, even more important than price or functions. And the Motorola brand cell phones, for the majority of the population, were seen as unappealing. The marketing challenge was to transform perceptions of the brand, making it cool, trendy, and stylish for the new generation of Chinese consumers.

A multidisciplinary group of about ninety people—"Team Moto"—comprising specialists in advertising, media, retail, PR, business consultancy, and digital, worked together to help make the brand's presentation coherent in all channels and at all touch points, from retail banners to websites to events. There wasn't a separate brand campaign. Perceptions of the brand were changed through product campaigns. This was no easy task because each cell phone had its own benefits. However, all communications shared a look, tone and feel that was unmistakably "Moto."

The unified look, tone, and feel helped a lot. It reassured prospective buyers they were joining a vigorous trend; the Chinese audience is both adventurous and conformist at the same time. The new campaign was based on the highly relevant creative idea of fashion, building on the growing desire for self-expression among people escaping drab conformity.

There was both creative innovation and the use of different media.

Digital, for example, had been underused. There are 500 million Internet users in China, more than in any other country. Motorola's online spending increased by 68 percent, against a category increase of 12 percent. One example was the launch of motomusic.com.cn, a legal music download site. It attracted over two million page views a day, and sales of the featured music phones (Razr and Rokr) grew by over 50 percent after the campaign.

Posters had also been underused. Around a third of Motorola's advertising spending went to posters, against a fifth for the leading competitor. The visual beauty of the campaign was best shown in posters, while for other brands, posters were merely a reminder medium.

Interactivity between on- and offline media was key. For instance, in the campaign for the Q phone, posters increased the effect of paid search by 44 percent. The combination of the posters and the search ad that got people to pay more attention to the Internet ad resulted in gold, silver, and bronze awards in the best use of new media category in the 2007 Asian Marketing Effectiveness Awards.

The combination of high profile creativity and innovative media produced a campaign that was much better known than would have been expected for the budget. Nokia spent $21 million more on advertising than Motorola in 2006, but ad awareness was practically identical: 77 percent for Nokia vs. 76 percent for Motorola.

Following the introduction of the Moto Tribes campaign at the end of 2005, Motorola's market share rose to 20 percent in 2006, an increase of 59 percent.

Motorola's success worldwide in 2006 was boosted by the RAZR, an extraordinarily popular product: Motorola has sold more Razrs than Apple has sold iPods. However, growth in China outstripped the global rate by a country mile. Much the same Motorola products are available in China as in the rest of the world, so product improvements cannot wholly explain China's exceptional performance.

Nor was price cutting solely responsible. Motorola was selling proportionately more of its less expensive phones as it expanded into the Chinese market, but it maintained a price premium over average phone prices in 2006. The econometric models used isolated advertising effects on sales (factoring out things such as price and promotion efforts) and proved the campaign was working. An example of advertising's immediate effect on sales was shown in the launch of the Q phone. The Q was available for pre-order in weeks 46–47 of 2007 and for sale generally in week 48. The online advertising campaign began in week 49. Once it started, page views increased by 1,750 percent, from 29,000 to 800,000 a week. With advertising, Q's sales rose to become six times higher than the leading competitor's. Our models showed that marketing expenditures as a whole created 26 percent of Motorola sales. Advertising was the main driver. It created 55 percent of those sales—that is, 14 percent of total sales while accounting for only 11 percent of total marketing spend. Another way of putting it is that each 10,000 yuan (the Chinese currency) spent on advertising sold 384 phones, while the same amount spent on promotion in the retail stores sold 96 phones. Assuming an average industry profit margin of around 30 percent per phone sold, advertising created some 15 yuan in profit for every yuan spent. This is a much higher return on marketing investment (ROMI) than from retail push.

Now, you may be wondering why we needed to go through all the effort required by econometric modeling. Couldn't we look at the individuals we communicated with, and see if they bought more of our product? We could, if they were using addressable media, which most digital media is these days. This approach, individual level attribution, has become an incredibly hot topic in digital advertising, where we actually know which individuals saw our advertising and can track whether they ultimately click on our banners or engage with our content afterward. (See our discussion in Chapter 4, where we talked about ways to find potential customers.) This type of individual level attribution is more accurate—you are looking at individuals rather than aggregated sales trends over time. It cannot, however, be used for traditional media. There simply is no perfect way to know if someone who saw one Honda ad on TV bought a Honda as a result. This is why we need econometric analysis to assess the performance of the entire media mix.

This diagram shows how individual level attribution works:

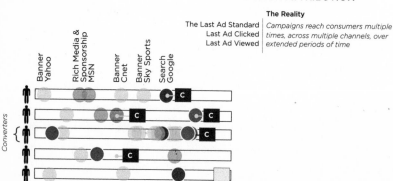

CONVERSION ATTRIBUTION

The Reality

The Last Ad Standard | *Campaigns reach consumers multiple*
Last Ad Clicked | *times, across multiple channels, over*
Last Ad Viewed | *extended periods of time*

Banner Yahoo

Rich Media & Sponsorship MSN

Banner Cnet

Banner Sky Sports

Search Google

Converters

You can see the "journeys" of five different consumers, the ones on the left. The first consumer (the one at the top) saw a banner ad on Yahoo!, a banner ad with rich media (something moves on the screen) and an ad on MSN.com, a banner on CNET, and a banner on Sky Sports. Then she searched on Google. The "C" stands for when each consumer clicked on the message to learn more or to buy.

Now here is the big question: What caused the consumer to take action? Was it the initial Yahoo! banner ad, the other banner ads, the rich media exposure, or was it search? Well, it was probably a combination of all. But knowing to what degree each piece of communication contributed to the sale is very important. If you attribute the entire sale to the last touch that happened before the sale, then search will probably get too much credit. This is what is called the "last click attribution" method. And this may surprise you: Despite the inherent fallacy, it is the one that most companies still use, because it is the easiest.

Let me illustrate the importance of the right attribution through the example of Caesars digital media business. We started working with them in late 2007, when the economy was slowing and vacancy rates at Caesars were climbing. Our challenge was to provide a charge to their online bookings business in the face of the looming recession and increased competition. Rigorous data collection and measurement techniques were instituted; and the results were quick and dramatic. Within one year, with the same media spending, Caesars doubled revenue generated from hotel bookings.

The attribution issue was tackled head-on. Many things were being done online—banner ads, rich media exposure, search, etc. The question was, Which approach was working best? We started from scratch and decided to mine the log level data provided by the adserving companies. (As we discussed in Chapter 4, every time you see or click a banner ad, the company responsible for serving up those banners tracks how you respond.)

When we mined these logs, we found that there was a "view-through" effect of over 40 percent that lasted as long as fifteen days. This means that 40 percent of the total revenue contribution of a banner campaign came from people who did not click on the banner initially but who still booked a room within fifteen days of when they had seen the banner. This was a very important finding! If we had looked only at the direct revenue generated by people clicking on the banner, we would have missed 40 percent of the sales it was producing. That could have led us to eliminate a campaign that was actually performing really well. (It also means that we were overcompensating other campaigns by wrongly attributing the revenue of the banner campaigns to them.)

In addition to looking at the indirect effects of banner campaigns, we also looked at cross-media effects. We found a 12 percent increase in search conversions after ad exposure. What's more, we found that certain placements had a higher impact on search behavior than others. This was important because when measured directly (getting credit only when they were the last ad seen before the sale), those placements appeared to be inefficient. This was especially true for ads on travel sites. People who saw banner ads on travel sites were much more likely to go and search for a Caesars hotel room on their own—in the attempt to find the best deal—instead of clicking on the ad and being taken to the Caesars website directly.

PUTTING IT ALL TOGETHER: UPS, A CASE STUDY

We have covered a lot of ground in this chapter. By now you know how to build a measurement plan and use multiple data sources to track performance. We have talked about how dashboards can give you a single view of how well you are doing. And we have shown some of the more advanced techniques that not only track performance metrics but also try and attribute the right proportion of success to specific actions. Now let's show how it all works in concert by looking at how one of Ogilvy's biggest clients, UPS, measures the performance of its marketing efforts.

UPS built its entire company on operational excellence. They optimize absolutely everything. For example, UPS trucks almost never take left turns. The company calculated that it could save millions of dollars each year by eliminating the time its drivers had to wait to make left turns, so making a left turn is done only if there is no òther option. With such focus on optimizing every aspect of their business, it's no surprise that UPS is at the cutting edge when it comes to measuring the performance of their communications budget.

I started working with UPS in the wake of the economic crisis of 2008 when they decided they needed a new long-term foundation for continued growth. Christine Owens, senior vice president of communications and brand management for UPS, was clear in her expectations. Communications was not a cost center but a true business driver accountable for measurable growth. Christine spent most of her career at UPS in operations, and she brings that rigor to communications. Aligning the brand strategy with the business strategy would be crucial. The company needed a way to communicate all the capabilities it had added in recent years, capabilities that took it far beyond shipping.

Our goal was to build deeper, more strategic relationships with clients and potential clients by getting them to consider UPS as a business partner, (you will see that the company could do just about anything for them). UPS knew that customers who used more of UPS's services spent more and were less likely to leave. Building deeper relationships with their customers would position UPS for the future.

After a long, complicated, and detailed pitch process— UPS doesn't leave anything to chance, especially picking their partners—during the summer and fall of 2009, UPS hired Ogilvy to tackle this challenge.

We set out to achieve the following objectives:

1. Strengthen the UPS brand and reposition UPS as a supplier of a broader range of services

2. Enable the sales force to sell more of UPS's services

3. Generate incremental shipping revenue

4. Inspire employees

Here are the insights that led to the strategy:

Most small and medium businesses (SBMs) aspire to be big companies and require a business partner, not just a shipper, to achieve that. Even though most of our sales to these companies would be in package shipping, just promoting package shipping was not the most appealing story to tell. Small and mid-market companies needed someone who could help them grow, expand across borders, be more efficient and productive. But this was not something they looked to a shipping company for help with. We'd have to let these customers know how UPS could help them. UPS had the breadth of services and solutions to be a strategic partner across a company's entire supply chain. They could stock and run the warehouse; they had the technology to clear the goods through customs, ship anything from small packages to air freight, handle the returns, and even do product repairs! UPS could make a customer's supply chain buzz with efficiency, which could make a business more competitive.

Small and medium businesses needed help with supply chain management (SCM), but the term "supply chain management" was seen as being the preserve of big companies. Despite the reality that they all had supply chains, SMBs did not relate to that language. They used words like "coordination," "logistics," and "planning." Some thought SCM was about stock location and warehousing, which didn't seem relevant to many, given their size. UPS could be *first* to define the complex series of processes that made commerce hum for the small and middle market. This was a huge opportunity. Especially since UPS, with its unique range of services, is the only company that can legitimately make this claim. UPS would be known as a resource SMBs could use to grow and expand their businesses.

But we needed to express this simply. We needed an expression that could articulate and popularize everything that UPS could do for businesses. We came up with the following idea: Let's take the ugly word "logistics," make it beautiful, and have UPS own it.

From the beginning it was clear that logistics was much more than an advertising idea like "99.44 percent pure." Logistics was a business idea that could transform not just how customers viewed UPS, but also how UPS employees viewed their own jobs.

Before we thought about creative ideas, we thought about what it really meant to set a new agenda in the business world. Tone would be critical. Logistics had to feel like an important and new concept in business, but it couldn't feel too intellectual or it would seem remote. The creative platform needed to be human.

We started with a simple theme that would guide everything: We Love Logistics. It reflected UPS's passion for delivering the logistics that would keep businesses competitive. We then developed a series of iconic graphic hearts, each designed to communicate a unique UPS capability from technology to sustainability and even healthcare.

We needed to get all this across to UPS employees as well, in order to reset how UPS thought of itself. So we started by taking the "We Love Logistics" message directly to the employees through a video message from the CEO who explained that this was the business that UPS had always been in, but that the company had never really defined it this way before.

Prestigious media outlets seeded the idea outside of the company. Webinars with the *Washington Post, New York Times,* and the *Harvard Business Review* exposed the power of the new logistics for growing businesses. We created a Logistics lounge within small business summits run by *GrowCo* and the *New York Times.* Long copy print ads defined the idea in detail. It was anything but traditional print. It was long-form print that read like a business article with a clear articulation of why the "New Logistics" was a force that could give growing businesses an edge. Television ads made logistics feel big, inspiring, and human. Enlisting UPS employees from around the globe and as well as customers, we created a song about Logistics to the tune of the Dean Martin classic *That's Amore.* It was designed to convey the complexity and power of the UPS logistics network in a way that felt simple and memorable.

Premium outdoor ads made the idea seem big, significant, and necessary. We wrapped subway stations and prominent buildings in high-traffic business areas, and dominated train stations with digital billboards while simultaneously blasting the We ♥ Logistics song throughout the station. We created an industry-segmented microsite that housed videos, articles, tools, and case studies that addressed specific issues across a range of key industries. The content was pushed through social media as well as paid channels that encouraged ongoing interaction and sharing.

So how did we find out whether this all worked? Well, we went back to the four objectives we established at the beginning of the process: strengthen the UPS reputation as a solutions provider, enable the sales force to sell more products, generate incremental income, and inspire employees.

In the table below you can see how we mapped them to metrics and to measurement sources. (Don't worry, I will define the measurement sources.)

OBJECTIVE	METRICS	MEASUREMENT SOURCE
Strengthen the UPS brand and reposition UPS as a supplier of a broader range of services	percentage of businesses recognizing UPS as a leader in logistics	brand tracker
	percentage of businesses agreeing that UPS offered a "broad range of services to meet business needs"	brand tracker
Enable the sales force to sell more of UPS's services	key indicators that we were broadening the conversation the sales people could have with their customers.	sales survey
Generate incremental shipping revenue	incremental shipping revenue attributed to the campaign	business impact study
Inspire employees	percentage of employees believed the campaign captured all the things UPS does	employee survey
	percentage who recognized that using logistics would help UPS compete and win new business	employee survey
	qualitative feedback	various sources

For the first objective we wanted to see that if we shifted perceptions of UPS, we thereby strengthened the UPS brand. We did this through two measurement sources. First we put in place a brand tracking study, which asked our target audience what their perceptions were of UPS. This allowed us to analyze shifts in perceptions over the period of the campaign. Within weeks of launch, 70 percent of small and medium businesses agreed UPS was a "leader in logistics." We also found out that 90 percent agreed that UPS offered a "broad range of services to meet business needs."

We measured overall brand strength using the BrandZ survey we mentioned in Chapter 3. This survey translates the pyramid scores we discussed there into a single metric of brand strength called Brand Voltage. This metric is proven to be highly predictive of future market-share growth. Just months after the logistics campaign launch, UPS's BrandZ Voltage score increased .142, indicating a 14.2 percent increase in the net probability that UPS would gain share in the following year.

The second objective of the campaign was to ensure that it supported UPS's sales force. We assessed performance against this objective by asking the sales force themselves. This was done through a sales-force survey. We found that the campaign made it easier for the majority of sales people to sell more UPS services and solutions.

The third objective was to increase revenues. Measuring the impact of communications efforts on sales is always tough in a business to business (B2B) environment. When a complex multimillion-dollar B2B deal gets closed, it is usually the result of a number of sales and marketing efforts. Brand advertising will probably have generated awareness and possibly consideration. The online experience, both on and off the brand's website, will have contributed as well. The initial lead might have come from Demand Generation tactics such as email, telemarketing, or direct mail, or perhaps through direct response TV or print. Public relations and peer reviews (including word-of-mouth) are likely to play an important role as well. The sales force will have worked on nurturing and closing the lead. Disentangling the contributions of all these activities to the ultimate sale is a real challenge. And in the case of UPS, that was just the media challenge. The nature of UPS's complex B2B environment made things exponentially more difficult on top of that because:

- Purchasing decisions in B2B are usually made by a number of people in a decision making unit (DMU). Finding a correlation between an individual's marketing exposure and the purchase decision made by the unit the individual belongs to is hard.

- Sales cycles in B2B tend to be longer. Months could go by between the marketing message and a purchase, which makes it especially difficult to disentangle the cause and effect over time.

- Because of the longer sales cycles, decision makers tend to get exposed to a high volume of different marketing messages before they make a purchase. This makes it harder to determine which message prompted them to buy.

- The sales force tends to play such a big role in the closing of deals that it often becomes impossible to observe a direct impact of marketing on B2B revenue.

Here is how we tackled the challenge. We worked out a new and innovative research methodology that matched UPS's brand-tracking survey to its sales. This allowed the company to see what happened to a customer's shipping volume for those who said they liked key brand attributes more after having seen an ad. Did they really go on and buy more products and services from UPS? This matching back to revenues also allowed UPS to follow the people whose attitudes changed during the couple of months since they were interviewed. The company can then perform statistical analysis to find the correlations between someone seeing an ad and someone changing her perceptions and ultimately buying more. UPS is able to analyze the sequence of events beginning with advertising exposure, then the willingness of a potential customer to take a UPS sales call or other actions that indicate a preparedness to buy, and finally to the ultimate purchase. While there is advanced modeling that goes on behind the scenes, the results are simple and intuitive and help quantify the interrelationships between the different mind-sets a customer goes through on the path to a purchase.

This analysis revealed that in just eight months the campaign drove more than *20 percent of UPS's overall incremental shipping revenue* among small- and middle-market companies.

The final objective of the campaign was to inspire the UPS employees. Here is where we used an employee survey to see how the campaign affected morale. We found that the campaign gave them a renewed sense of pride and purpose. Some 84 percent of employees believed the campaign captured all the things UPS does; 77 percent recognized that using logistics, instead of price, would help UPS compete and win new business. We also gathered more qualitative feedback from the employees.

UPS not only demonstrated the effectiveness of the campaign through the techniques described above, they also put in place continuous tracking mechanisms that allowed them to read preliminary results of their campaign very quickly. The UPS Live dashboard was essential to this. The dashboard gave more than fifty users access to real time results from the campaigns. The dashboard was web-enabled and gave different users secure access to the results with customized views. It integrates eighty-one different data sources, providing more than 300 metrics across every channel UPS used in the campaign. It also included investment data, allowing UPS to monitor the ROI of their tactics in real time. And it provided the teams with an important unified data source ensuring everyone is looking at the same data. The facts gathered from all the sources described above showed that ultimately, the Logistics campaign did a lot more than help UPS meet its incremental revenue objectives. It has positioned UPS for the future.

THINGS TO DO MONDAY MORNING

1. *It all starts with figuring out what you need to measure.* Look at your goals. Figure out what it will take to achieve them, and tie metrics to each and every one of the steps. Then formulate how you are going to track those measures so that you stay on track.

2. *With your plan established . . .* go and find the data you need. (This chapter supplied you with a wide range of potential sources.)

3. *Once you have all the data,* put it together in a marketing dashboard (a simple Excel spreadsheet or a more advanced solution, depending on what you are looking for). Once you have whatever you want to use in place, you are ready to track and optimize.

CHAPTER SEVEN

OPTIMIZE: HOW DO YOU DO MORE OF WHAT WORKS AND LESS OF WHAT DOESN'T?

Optimization—improving your marketing efforts through analysis and testing—is not a one-off event. It's a cycle of continuous improvement in which you measure, analyze, optimize, and then measure, analyze, and optimize again and again. An important part of what we are going to discuss will include how you can implement processes that make sure you always continue to improve your performance. Along the way, you will learn why your sexy little numbers can even be your creatives' best friends, helping them develop market messages that customers really want to hear. Companies become increasingly better through the subsequent iterations of the cycle. Some of them become a lot better over time. Why? Because they have a process that allows them to do so.

Process, to some, is a dirty word; but it can help to get the basics right and it is simply more efficient to institutionalize a disciplined approach to ensure that the best way of doing things is implemented and followed.

Best practices, when it comes to our Sexy Little Numbers, aren't difficult; the catch is, you need to *do* them. This is where a process has really helped one of our global technology clients. We noticed that while they were doing very sophisticated work to measure their advertising, they weren't when it came to their direct marketing.

So we put in place what we call the A2A—Analysis to Action—framework that resulted in $100 million in increased revenues for them.

Graphically the framework looks like this:

ANALYSIS

The obvious starting point is data. What often happens—as you know—is that the data you need is in different places. In the old days, to implement A2A for large clients we had to use hundreds of spreadsheets that had been created from scores of different databases, which meant we were soon in Excel Hell. It is not a pretty place. When you are there, there is nothing to do other than manually stitch together those multiple spreadsheets into one giant one, which invariably will crash the day before your report is due.

Doing all this is incredibly time-consuming. And moving all those numbers from one place to another also results in a lot of mistakes by even the best and most meticulous analyst. And chances of making mistakes increase dramatically when a lot of manual work is involved.

Today, this can be easily avoided by writing software programs to automate the manual tasks. That way the work is only done once—when the programmer writes the software code. From there on out, it is automated and error free. I have seen one programmer replace as many as ten people who were doing the work manually. This is what we did for our global tech client. Not only did it dramatically cut down the cycle times and increase the accuracy of the data, it meant we could spend more time analyzing the information we had.

In the analysis stage, you figure out what worked and what didn't. We would constantly reexamine the data based on new questions that were generated by our clients, creatives, planners, account managers, or analysts. Once a new question came up, we would formulate the hypothesis and then find the data from the campaigns we had run in the past to validate or reject the hypothesis.

Here's an example. Since our client's products are often complex, they run a lot of webcasts that explain them in more detail. In order to view the webcast, the viewer needs to complete a form that gives her contact details to the client so that a salesperson can follow up.

One hypothesis was that the length of the webcast had an impact on the registration rate (the percentage of all people invited to the webcast by email who actually complete the registration form). More specifically, the thought was that webcasts of more than an hour would have a lower registration rate. We analyzed the historical data and indeed found that this was the case. The shorter webcasts had more than double the registration rate of webcasts of more than an hour. This led to the mandate that no webcasts should be longer than an hour.

Pretty simple stuff but very impactful, given the sheer volume of webcasts the client puts in the market every year.

The point here is, you can test everything. For example:

- Does one kind of offer work better at a different point in the sales cycle than another? Test it during both to find out.

- Does an energy saving calculator generate more leads than offering a free energy audit. Test both and look at the results.

- Sure, what you have might be working, but would something else boost sales by 2 percent? There is no way to find out for sure unless you test.

Companies that don't do much testing tend to say it delays things. They see it as extra work that doesn't generate much in the way of interesting insights.

But testing can be fun. Experimentation can be fun, and testing *is* experimentation. It's all about trying out new things to see if they work. If they do, then you can roll them out on a broader scale. For the tech client, for example, we initially started to run what people call *A/B tests*; if you substitute the word *or* for the slash between *A* and *B*, you will instantly understand how they work.We constantly test new ideas for the client. We formulate a hypothesis and then put a test in market to validate or reject it. For example, would giving someone an option to click on "Learn more" to gain more information improve the response rate to an email? The answer, we learned, was an overwhelming yes. In this case, the "call to action" increased the performance of the email by 50 percent. Small changes can make big differences, as we will see throughout this chapter.

You can get extremely granular with this. For example, we test the subject lines of emails. Subject lines are very important since they are the only thing you see when an email enters your mailbox. They determine whether you will open it or not. So there is a real art in writing great subject lines. We inform that art by our science. Our tests show time and again that shorter subject lines work better. And we also learned that the length of the subject line matters less if you put the important information at the beginning.

Action!

The first three bubbles of the A2A framework—data, analyze, test—focus on "Analysis." The last two—execute, share—is where "Action" comes into play. The first step toward action is sharing the knowledge gathered through all campaigns that have been analyzed and all the tests that have been run. For a tech client we instigated monthly A2A calls where all people around the world who were responsible for direct marketing would get together and discuss the results of their tests. We would also review the test pipeline.

The test pipeline can be a very valuable management tool. It looks like this:

	LIST	OFFER	CADENCE	INTERACTIVE	EMAIL
EBF	Internal External List Testing		DM vs EM vs Both (3Q)		
EP	Messaging by Segment Test (??)				Subject Line Test
DTA	HTML vs Text by Segment Test (3G)				Create Version Test
LI					
GRM				Lending Page Optimization	
OIT	Blades Propersity Model				
R&G					HTML vs Email Test (????)
MM					
CIO				Landing Page/ Banner Ad Testing	
LOB					

This grid shows which tests are being discussed, which have been executed, which have been postponed, and which are completed. The columns show the main learning areas we have identified and places where we wanted to get more intelligence. The rows show the different campaigns we ran.

EXECUTION

The last and probably most important part of the A2A cycle is execution. This is where getting things right in the first four stages will really help. They are all designed to make life easier and to increase awareness of tests and the improvements they can bring.

The point here is simple: You can do all the analyzing, testing, and sharing you want; but if it doesn't change the way you execute, it will make no difference. Ultimately it is up to the person who runs the campaigns to execute based on what has been learned.

Most of the recommendations that come out of the A2A framework are very tactical and may seem small. However, when these incremental improvements are extrapolated across a volume of activities, they can add up to significant sums. For example, our client estimated that the effect of implementing all the best practices derived from the A2A framework one year led to an *increase of $100 million in revenues the next year* "simply" by improving dozens of small things such as, to name just one, optimizing the subject line in emails (which leads to more of them being opened, which in turn leads to higher sales). All these little changes led to a huge payoff.

With the basics of an A2A program covered, let's go into more detail on the analysis and testing stages, and in the process give some examples of how we have helped companies optimize their communications. Let's first look at how data can help improve the creative product, and then examine some more advanced ways of testing in the digital world. We will finish things off with a case study of TD Ameritrade, a client that has really excelled at optimizing its campaigns.

CREATIVE FEEDBACK

It's not easy to sell people on the idea that analytics can be a catalyst for creative freedom. I have been doing analytics in the "creative" environment of a communications agency for quite a while and know that when analytics and creative are thrown in the mix together, it's not always a happy marriage.

Creative people often see the discipline of analytics as an ROI-focused approach that judges the quality of new ideas by looking backward rather than forward and in doing so advocating the status quo and standing in the way of innovation. Analysts test new thinking to death with endless focus groups and market research. Because of these perceptions, analytics is often seen as an obstacle to new ideas and the enemy of "true" creativity, and even "soulless."

I agree that testing (or any form of data-driven design) can be counterproductive if you don't learn from the past. Obsessive testing can slow down the creative process. There are design and communications principles that have been around for a long time. They don't necessarily need to be tested over and over again. Experts familiar with them should be given the authority to overrule overeager data analysts. A test management system can help here. The system usually includes the following basic components:

Testing history. Findings from previous tests should be consistently documented so they can be stored in an insight repository. At the very minimum, this can be a simple spreadsheet that lists all tests that have run in the past, their objective, hypothesis, and outcome. You never want to reinvent the wheel.

Testing briefing. Every test should have a briefing document that outlines the testing hypothesis, the test design, the timing, the anticipated benefit, cost, and ROI. This detailed briefing document will standardize the inputs required to build the testing history and pipeline.

Testing pipeline. The testing pipeline keeps track of all the tests that are being planned and are under way. Depending on the number of tests you run, and the complexity of your organization, this can be captured in anything from a simple spreadsheet that lists all planned tests with a short description, timeline, and status to a system that is managed through sophisticated campaign management platforms.

Guidelines. Storing the results of past tests in an insights repository is not enough. The findings need to be aggregated and written up as guidelines that are communicated throughout the organization. Again, tried and tested principles do not need to be tested over and over again.

Testing prioritization. New tests can be prioritized based on what we know already (through testing history and guidelines), what we have in the testing pipeline, and what the potential ROI could be from the rollout. Prioritization of tests will prevent excessive testing.

Despite the complaints from some creatives, I don't know many companies that test too much. The opposite is usually the case. Most companies' creative decisions don't live or die by the sword of data; they are based on often very subjective expert opinions or, even worse, on what web analytics author Avinash Kaushik calls the Hippo—the Highest Paid Person's Opinion.

This means companies tend to leave millions of dollars on the table. They don't test new ideas and fail to build up a body of knowledge of what works and what doesn't. A testing management system will help these companies as well. It can identify knowledge gaps and areas where mandatory tests are required.

And it can institutionalize testing by making it an integral part of the creative process. Of all analytical tools that can fuel better creative work, none is more powerful than testing, especially in the digital world.

TESTING IN A DIGITAL WORLD

We briefly demonstrated the principles of testing with UPS. But the A2A approach can be implemented everywhere, especially in the digital channels, where the possibilities for testing seem almost endless. Consider Kodak. We tried to improve the home page of the Kodak Online Store through implementing a test. Below you can find the original home page we wanted to optimize. Kodak didn't perceive any problems. They simply wanted to see if they could improve it.

We created six different pages to evaluate. So, rather than an A/B test, this was an A/B/C/D/E/F test. The one on page 201 tested best and generated an 11.3 percent increase in revenue, just by changing the layout.

The downside of this approach was that while we knew which page performed best, we didn't manage to isolate exactly what was driving the difference. I will show some techniques later that help pinpoint the exact changes that make a difference. But before I do, let me pause here to underscore an important point.

Testing will take the subjectivity and opinions out of the decision making. You may have liked one of the Kodak layouts, and I may have liked another, but the testing will tell us who is right. Rather than discussing iterations and versions based on best practices, experience, or simply taste, we can just try them out and let analytics be the judge of what works best. End of discussion.

Hopefully you will have started to see the power of optimization by now; but if you still need convincing, I will now show you how President Obama might have won the 2008 election through the clever use of our sexy little numbers. On page 202 you can see two versions of the Obama.com home page that ran during the election.

The one on the left is the original home page. In 2007 Dan Siroker was working at Google when Obama visited the Google campus in Mountain View. Dan was so inspired by Obama's chat that he gave up his job at Google, packed his bags for Chicago, and joined the Obama team. He didn't have a place to stay initially, so he slept on the floor of a friend's apartment. Dan ended up running the new media analytics team for the campaign. Overall, Obama raised $656 million, some $500 million of which came through online channels. The main online channel was the Obama.com page shown above.

Let me do a bit of foreshadowing. Dan and his team used some of the techniques I will describe later in this chapter to change the home page from the one on the left to the one on the right. There are only two changes involved. He changed the visual and he changed the button from "sign up" to "learn more." The effects of these two simple changes were game changing, as is shown in the table below.

	EMAIL SUBSCRIPTIONS	VOLUNTEERS	AMOUNT RAISED
Original	7,120,000	712,000	$143,000,000
New	10,000,000	1,000,000	$200,000,000
	+2,880,000	+288,000	+$57,000,000

The new Obama.com home page outperformed the original page by more than 40 percent. This resulted in 288,000 extra volunteers and $57 million in additional funds (or more than 25 percent of what Obama's opponent, John McCain, was able to raise *in total online*).

Dan Siroker didn't use just A/B testing or even A/B/C/D/E/F testing. He used multivariate testing, which is especially powerful in the digital world, where this type of advanced testing can be automated.

I first saw automated multivariate testing in action in 2002. By then I was running Ogilvy's global analytics knowledge community, and part of my job was organizing an annual conference where our analytics people from all over the world would get together to share best practices and discuss how we could further develop our analytics offerings. I was working in London at the time. The dollar was weak, and we decided to have the conference in Miami. I had never been to Miami and frankly didn't really expect much from it. Florida doesn't have a really great image in Europe, but I was very pleasantly surprised. It really had an interesting vibe and I was surprised by all the cool Art Deco architecture. I ran this conference in tandem with Nigel Howlett, a veteran in direct and data-based marketing. Nigel is a rather flamboyant British country gentleman and a phenomenal swimmer, as I learned the hard way. He managed to win $50 from me by betting that he would be able to swim 25 lengths of the National Hotel's famous 100-meter pool. (The bet occurred after we had a few drinks at the bar.) I still clearly remember him getting in the pool and then watching his gray head go up and down in the pool, doing one 100-meter length after another for what seemed like two hours!

In addition to being skilled in hustling bar bets, Nigel had a fine nose for finding interesting companies and new technologies. He invited an Australian company called Memetrics to the conference, and they demonstrated their automated multi-variate testing technology during our meeting and blew us all away with their eBay case.

EBay had asked Memetrics to optimize their pages using Memetrics' technology. Below you can see a representative page.

The first thing Memetrics did was identify the main areas they would test. This is shown in the diagram below. In this case, there are six content areas Memetrics would play around with.

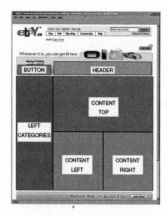

The second step was to develop different versions for every content block.

Memetrics created another four versions for the left categories, the content top, the content left, and the content right.

Now if you were to combine all these different versions, you would end up with 4,096 possible combinations or 4,096 slightly different web pages. Memetrics had developed a technology that would serve up those 4,096 different landing pages during the period when they ran the test to see which worked best.

After a couple of weeks, they were able to pick out the winning combination and measure the lift it generated. Below you can see the initial page (the control) and the optimized page. The winner showed a double-digit increase in the conversion rate, the number of visitors who came to the site and actually bought something (as opposed to just browsing). The conversion rate is expressed as a ratio: buyers divided by total visitors (which includes those who buy and those who don't).

Control Page   **Memetrics Optimal Page**

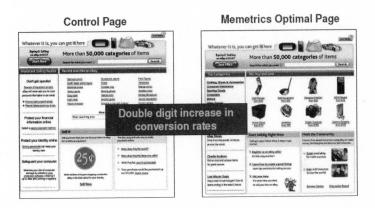

Double digit increase in conversion rates

Our reaction? This was testing on steroids, and we wanted in. In traditional direct mail, the analyst would have had to design the test manually and it would have been virtually impossible to have that many combinations. Memetrics had automated the entire process; and with the vast volumes of data that are being captured online, the possibilities seemed endless. The consulting firm Accenture later bought Memetrics.

We started using the technology with our clients and have had tremendous success. Later in this chapter, I will walk you through a case study of how we used multivariable testing for TD Ameritrade. Today, many web analytics vendors offer this technology, making multivariate testing much more common. It has almost turned it into a commodity. Google put its version, Google Site Optimizer (GSO), out in the market a few years ago, and it is free! So there is no excuse now for not testing, even using the most sophisticated way of testing, on your website.

Google's GSO shows you the results of your tests in real time. Below you can see a screenshot of the Obama GSO experiment.

Combinations (24)	Page Sections (2)			Download: XML CSV TSV	Print	
Disable	All Combinations (24) ▼ Key: ■ Winner ■ Inconclusive ■ Loser ?					
Combination	Status ?	Est. conv. rate ?		Chance to Beat Orig. ?	Observed Improvement ?	Conv./Visitors ?
Original	Enabled	8.26% ± 0.5%		—	—	1088 / 13167
☆ Top high-confidence winners. Run a follow-up experiment »						
Combination 11	Enabled	11.6% ± 0.6%		100%	40.6%	1504 / 12947
Combination 7	Enabled	10.3% ± 0.6%		100%	24.0%	1340 / 13073
Combination 3	Enabled	9.80% ± 0.6%		99.7%	18.7%	1277 / 13025
Combination 10	Enabled	9.23% ± 0.6%		95.9%	11.7%	1203 / 13031
Combination 8	Enabled	9.03% ± 0.6%		91.6%	9.28%	1178 / 13046
Combination 9	Enabled	8.77% ± 0.6%		81.8%	6.10%	1111 / 12672
Combination 6	Enabled	8.64% ± 0.5%		75.3%	4.58%	1108 / 12822

In the first column, you can see all the different combinations that are being tested. The little graph shows in real time which combination is winning. It's as if you are watching a horse race. I have found myself staring at this screen while running live tests, which is not necessarily very productive. But I can't help it. It's highly addictive.

In the second table, you can see which elements of the test

are determining its success. As you can see, the Learn More button and Family Image both outperformed the original.

				Chance to Beat Orig. ?	Observed Improvement ?	Conv./Visitors ?
Combinations (24)	**Page Sections (2)**		Download: XML CSV TSV | Print			
Relevance Rating ?	Variation	Est. conv. rate ?		Chance to Beat Orig. ?	Observed Improvement ?	Conv./Visitors ?
Button	Original	7.51% ± 0.2%		—	—	5851 / 77858
5 / 5	Learn More	8.91% ± 0.2%		100%	18.6%	6927 / 77729
	Join Us Now	7.62% ± 0.2%		73.5%	1.37%	5915 / 77644
	Sign Up Now	7.34% ± 0.2%		13.7%	-2.38%	5660 / 77151
Media	Original	8.54% ± 0.2%		—	—	4425 / 51794
5 / 5	Family Image	9.66% ± 0.2%		100%	13.1%	4996 / 51696
	Change Image	8.87% ± 0.2%		92.2%	3.85%	4595 / 51790
	Barack's Video	7.76% ± 0.2%		0.04%	-9.14%	3992 / 51427
	Sam's Video	6.29% ± 0.2%		0.00%	-26.4%	3261 / 51864
	Springfield Video	5.95% ± 0.2%		0.00%	-30.3%	3084 / 51811

THE DIGITAL PLAYGROUND

By now it must be clear that the possibilities for optimizing your communications in the digital world are endless. This can make digital an ideal playground for experimentation. What you learn can then be applied in off-line communications. Digital becomes the lab for the entire communications mix because there is so much data, it is cheap to test different versions, and you get the results back in minutes—days at the most—rather than the months it can take when we are working in the off-line world.

Here's an example of what you can learn. An analysis of online advertising for the Caesars hotel chain showed that the vast majority of *all* bookings were generated by online banners for Caesars and not the chain's other hotels. Since the ad actually took customers to the central reservation page, they explored the chain's other properties (Paris Las Vegas, Harrah's, Bally's, etc.) as well. Caesars seemed to have a magnetic effect for the entire Caesars portfolio. When we tested TV commercials that featured Caesars in one region, we found out that bookings in that region increased 12 percent *for all brands*. We used that insight to optimize our TV campaigns beefing up the role Caesars played in our advertising. This is a great example of how what happens in the digital world can help optimize more traditional campaigns.

Soon all channels will be digital. Google now gives you the ability to buy TV spots through an online interface. They have made buying TV so easy that anyone can do it. When you buy TV spots through Google TV, you get a taste of how much data is being gathered on the set-top boxes (which connect to your cable or satellite TV provider) in your living room. Google TV allows you to look at "tune out" data, for example. This can give advertisers an idea of how many people are tuning out of an ad. We have used that data to optimize some of our clients' TV spots.

Not surprisingly, the majority of people who tune out an ad—by changing the channel—do so within the first seconds of the commercial. After that initial spike, the number of viewers who tune out gradually declines during the length of the spot. That's the typical pattern.

But we noticed, in a particular Allstate ad, there was a second spike about 16 seconds into the commercial. This was exactly when a fairly aggressive call to action was introduced. This immediately helped us smooth the transition from informational to selling and reduce tune-out.

LET'S PUT IT ALL TOGETHER: TD AMERITRADE

We have walked through a number of techniques you can use to optimize your communications. Now, let's see how they can all work together by studying TD Ameritrade (TDA), a company that has been at the forefront of optimization for years.

Jim Dravillas, formerly of Ogilvy, now head of advertising research at Google, is a pioneer in digital analytics, and he is responsible for a lot of the work described in this chapter. From the day I met him, he has been at the forefront of how you can use analytical skills to make online marketing efforts more effective. Some of his best work was for TD Ameritrade, the online broker.

TDA is continually an early adopter of new technology because they have an ideal business model for analytics. They are primarily focused on growing the number of accounts. This means they run their entire business pretty much based on two metrics: the number of accounts they acquire and the cost per acquisition (CPA).

They also operate in a nearly "closed loop" system, where they know exactly which individuals they are communicating with and whether or not those people ultimately open up an account. This means it is relatively easy to determine the cause and effect of different marketing activities.

One of the first things Jim did for TDA was to implement an automated frequency capping tool, which is exactly what it sounds like. When you go to CNN.com and see a TDA ad, you may or may not click on it. When you see it two or three times, you might be more likely to click on it (maybe you didn't see it, or weren't paying attention, the first time it was served to you). However, if TDA shows you their ad twenty-five times and you still haven't clicked on it, it's fair to assume that you never will. You are not interested in TDA. TDA would save money by serving up that next impression to someone else. You have reached a saturation point after which it makes no more sense for TDA to serve the ad to you.

The trick, of course, is to determine that saturation point. Is it seeing the ad twenty-five, fifteen, or thirty-five times? And is it the same for everyone? This is where Jim comes in. He developed statistical models that estimate the saturation point based on characteristics of the ad, the placement (CNN.com or some other site) and your historical browsing behavior. And not only did he calculate the saturation point, he developed a way to automatically make sure you would no longer see a TDA ad once you reached it. They then took that extra money and used it to send ads to somebody else. Lead generation went up 15 percent (with a zero increase in the marketing budget).

Another vehicle Jim built was the automated creative rotation tool (I told him he needs a snappier name for it, but that's not the sort of thing Jim worries about). A company like TDA usually has a number of creative executions running simultaneously. Jim's tool analyzes the performance of each in real time and then integrates those findings into the company's ad server so that it *automatically* serves up more impressions of the creative that works and fewer of those that don't. After implementing this tool, TDA saw the lead generation rate jump 25 percent to 35 percent! (Again, with no increase in the marketing budget.)

Not only did this make the online advertising a lot more effective, it also gave the creative teams almost immediate feedback. Jim gave them reports that showed which color schemes worked best, which shapes, which visuals, which words, etc. The creative teams loved this information. They finally got real-time feedback on their work. This allowed them to experiment with new things and immediately see how their experiments performed. Jim had turned the digital ecosystem into the experimentation lab described earlier.

Another great example was the "day-parting" analysis, where we looked at what times of day were most favorable to advertise online. That's how granular you can get in the digital world; you can look at performance by hour! When we did this analysis, we saw that the prospects we brought in during the last hour of the trading day were much more likely to be of high value; that is, they tended to have a greater net worth and were more likely to manage their money through TDA. This led to the media strategy of "owning" the last hour of the trading day. We bought all media space on a number of big sites like CNNMoney and Yahoo! Finance during the final hour of trading. This campaign generated 15 percent more high-value customers than any other campaign we had ever run! This is a great example of how insights derived from data can spark creative ideas.

A GREAT LANDING

One of my favorite pieces of work Jim performed for TDA was the optimization of their landing page. When someone clicked on the TDA banners, they would see the page below.

TDA then hoped that the consumer would click on the "Apply Online Now" at the top right of the page. This would start the enrollment process.

Now TDA can spend all the money in the world to get people to this page, but if visitors don't click on the orange button and complete the enrollment process, TDA will not see a single dollar in return. You can just imagine how important this page is to the effectiveness of the marketing efforts. Jim knew this would be the perfect place to apply Memetrics (he had seen them in Miami as well—and he also lost money on Nigel's bet). He began by experimenting with the areas on the periphery of the page.

The creative teams developed a couple of versions for each of the four modules on the page we optimized, specifically:

- Client login button:
    o version 1: current
    o version 2: an offer
    o version 3: information about the enrollment process

- "Visit TDAMERITRADE.COM" link:
    o version 1: "Visit TDAMERITRADE.COM"
    o version 2: "Visit our main site"
    o version 3: no link

- "Apply Online Now" button text:
    o version 1: "Apply Online Now"
    o version 2: "Open your account"
    o version 3: "Get Started"

- "Apply Online Now" button color:
    o version 1: green
    o version 2: blue
    o version 3: orange

- Offer space at bottom:
    o Version 1: 1 rotating offer. The offer changes every time someone visits the page.

o version 2: 3 offers

o version 3: 4 offers

If you combine all these different options, you get 243 slightly different landing pages. Jim worked with Memetrics and put these 243 pages online for a period of fifteen days. The technology made sure that if you came to the site more than once, you would always see the same version. After fifteen days, Jim picked the page that performed best. Below you can see the page we started with (on the right) next to the one that performed best in the experiment (on the left).

And it didn't just perform better, it did a lot better! The conversion rate on the page increased 15 percent. That means that for every 100 people coming to the landing page, 15 more opened an account. The ROI on the test was 43:1!

If you compare the two pages above, you can see that they are very similar; it was the subtle differences that paid huge dividends. The table on page 214 shows what we changed. For example, the green button worked better than the orange button. This usually surprises people. Orange stands out, so most people assume that works better. It's true, orange does stand out. But it also signals "Danger!" Green is more inviting.

ATTRIBUTE	CONTROL	OPTIMAL
Button Style	Orange	**Green**
Button Text	"Apply online now"	**"Get Started"**
TDA Text Link	"Visit tdameritrade.com"	**"Visit our main site"**
Client Login Link	Is Present	**Is Present**
Promotional Banners	4 Banners	**Single rotating banner**

15% INCREASE IN CONVERSION — **43:1 ROI** ON THE TEST

"Get Started" beat "Apply Online Now." "Apply Online Now" is more aggressive, and "Get started" is more inviting (we saw the same trend with Obama's home page, where "Learn more" worked better than "Sign up now"). The single rotating banner outperformed the four static boxes that made an offer. This is a great example of the negative effect of clutter. Most companies want to put as many offers on a page as possible, hoping one will interest the consumer. But less is more in this case.

Long-Term Benefits

Jim worked with TDA for ten years and the graph on page 215 clearly demonstrates the power of his continuous optimization efforts. The graph displays the two metrics TDA uses to run its business. The vertical bars show the number of accounts the company acquired every year. The jagged horizontal line is the cost per acquisition.

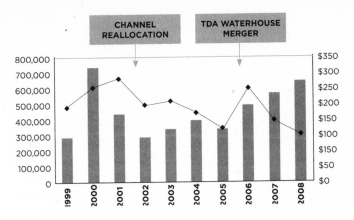

Jim started working with TDA in 1999 during the dot-com boom. You can see how the volume of accounts grew. Unfortunately, so did the CPA. When the bubble burst, TDA saw its acquisition levels drop and it could no longer afford the high CPA. At that moment, Jim used his analytical skills to radically change the media mix, taking dollars out of expensive network television channels and putting them into more cost-efficient digital channels and direct response television (DRTV), ads that ask consumers to respond directly to the company. An infomercial is one example of a DRTV ad. At the same time, we started using the tools described above—automated creative rotation, frequency capping, day-parting analysis, and multivariate site optimization. The CPA went down dramatically while TDA maintained and in the last years even increased the volume of accounts.

In 2005 Ameritrade merged with TD Waterhouse. As a result, the volume of accounts increased as you can see in the chart above. Unfortunately, their acquisition efforts were a lot less effective, as is demonstrated by the stark increase of the CPA. But from 2006 onward, you can see how Jim and his team managed to drive down that CPA again through daily optimization.

THINGS TO DO MONDAY MORNING

1. *Just do it.* Acquire the discipline of testing. Use the A2A framework constantly. Never stop formulating new hypotheses to test.

2. *Test in digital.* This is where testing is cheap and fast. You should experiment with multivariate testing tools. Google Site Optimizer is free!

3. *Use digital as your lab.* This means you need to apply what you have learned in digital everywhere.

CHAPTER EIGHT

THE FUTURE

Here's a bold prediction, but one I am confident in making: Most of the marketing, research, advertising, and support functions associated with how we try to increase sales today will be very different—or even eliminated—within our lifetimes. That's how much of a difference analytics will make. Specifically, all those functions (and more) will be **automated**: automatic testing, automated creative rotation (where and how often ads appear), and automated targeting. There also will be automated real-time buying of advertising and marketing time and space. And decisions about how much to pay to reach those specific customers will be made automatically as well.

What will people do? There will be only two kinds of jobs: "technicians," the folks who make sure the automation runs smoothly, and "magicians," the people who take advantage of all the tools available to create and implement ideas that boost sales and earnings dramatically. If you are in the business, you had best figure out today which one you want to be.

Hopefully by now you have a clear view on how data can help you today with the daily business decisions you need to make and, in the process, transform your business. But what about the future?

Predictions are always tricky. (We still are not commuting to work by jet packs, as they promised us years ago.) But there are a few reasonable assumptions that can prepare you for what's ahead.

We've covered how we got here but what happens next?

Future Trends

The digital data deluge. Here's an interesting statistic: It is estimated that all the words ever spoken by human beings could be stored in approximately 5 exabytes* of data. At the close of 2010, worldwide storage needs for all forms of data occupied close to 1,000 exabytes. That's a tremendous amount of data!! The bulk of this data is—and will continue to be—generated through digital media of all kinds, and the numbers will only increase dramatically, since, as we discussed, just about everything will become digital. This means there will be even more data for marketers to use. Google estimates that by 2020 we will generate 53 zettabytes[†] of data.

The techniques currently used for identifying the most valuable individuals to target will soon be able to be applied to pretty much every element of the media mix. TV will become addressable, so that you will be able to target certain viewers without wasting your money on others. The majority of print advertising will be consumed on digital devices—think iPads, Kindles, and improved smart phones—and the same will be true for radio. This means we will be able to target individuals based on how valuable we think they are.

As more of their interactions move to digital platforms,

---

[*]For the math geeks among us, the following description is based on information provided by SearchStorage.com: An exabyte is a large unit of computer data storage; the prefix *exa-* means one billion billion, or one quintillion. More precisely, it is two to the sixtieth power, or 1,152,921,504,606,846,976 bytes. In decimal terms, an exabyte is a billion gigabytes. An exabyte of storage could contain 50,000 years' worth of DVD-quality video.

[†]We knew you'd ask. Again, courtesy of SearchStorage.com: A zettabyte is a measure of storage capacity and is two to the seventieth power bytes or one sextillion bytes. There are a thousand exabytes in a zettabyte.

consumers will also leave behind much more data about what they are interested in, since they will be visiting sites and consuming media that captures everything they do. This will give advertisers the opportunity to get to know them much better so we can tailor our offers and products accordingly.

Increased visibility into how consumers interact with your brand will also increase opportunities for interacting with them. We have seen the shift already. Marketing today is a lot less one-way and much more about engaging consumers through conversations, relationships, interactive entertainment, etc. This tends to involve many more interactions between consumer and brand, which again generates a lot more data.

That's the good news. The bad news is not all of this interaction is happening within a company's control. Most companies have spent millions of dollars over the last decade or so to create single customer views. As we discussed earlier, these SCVs are databases that capture all the information that is generated when customers interact with the brand directly through a platform the company controls—point of sale, call centers, corporate websites, and the like.

Increasingly, though, these interactions are happening on external platforms such as social networks, search engines, and advertising networks. The data generated on these platforms does not necessarily flow into companies' traditional single customer views. This means that a lot of companies will need to rethink the concept of the SCV. It will be hard for them to create internal systems that are flexible enough to keep up with the latest new platform that becomes popular. (Yesterday it was Twitter; today it's Foursquare. I don't know what will be next, but I do know that soon there will be a new platform that has gained critical mass.)

To deal with this, we will see the emergence of third-party

data houses that will be able to integrate all the information gathered on these new platforms and resell it to companies that can then append the information to their corporate data warehouses. This is already starting to happen with the emergence of the data management platforms (DMPs) we discussed in Chapter 4. We might even see the emergence of data exchanges—marketplaces where data is sold and the price is set based on the laws of supply and demand.

What Should You Pay for Data?

The buying and selling of data about consumers has been going on for a long time. But what really determines the value (and therefore the price) of that information? There are three drivers: predictive power, recency, and exclusivity.

1. *Predictive power.* Let's say, for example, that I am a manufacturer of drills and I am trying to purchase data that will help me identify whether a consumer is interested in buying one. And let's assume that I can choose between the following two sets of information.

SET 1	SET 2
Number of hours spent on DIY per week	Number of vacations taken per year
Number of hammers owned	Interest in water sports
Size of the house owned	Age

Most people would agree that the data points in Set 1 are more valuable for a drill manufacturer than those in Set 2. This is because of their natural correlation with someone's likelihood to purchase drills.

That example is very straightforward. However, if you had to determine the Predictive Power of one hundred different data points, you would have to build statistical models that predict the likelihood of someone buying a drill based on all one hundred data points.

Whether you build statistical models or not, the principle is that data points with a high predictive power will improve our ability to predict whether a consumer will be interested in buying a drill, and, that as a drill manufacturer, I am prepared to pay a higher price for them.

2. *Recency.* I especially want to draw your attention to this point, because it is going to become progressively more important. In a digital world people often reveal in real time what their intentions are. Knowing whether a person has searched for drills on Google, whether he has clicked on a banner ad for drills, or whether he has seen a drill-related video online today can be very powerful. These data points generally outperform the more traditional data points that are listed in Set 1 in the example on page 220 because they are direct indications of a consumer's interests and needs at a certain point in time. This is why recency is very important. When someone searches for a drill on Google, this is very valuable information, *if I can target that person immediately.* Knowing someone searched for a drill three months ago in and of itself is a lot less valuable. The predictive power of self-disclosed data points starts to decline minutes after the observed event. Because of the disproportionately high value of very recent data, I anticipate most of the future innovation will focus on capturing multiple events in real time and shortening the cycles between observed events and the ability to use that knowledge for targeting.

3. *Exclusivity.* The final driver is exclusivity. Let's assume that I can buy only the data points in Set 1. Let's also assume that I have built a statistical model and have determined that the general predictive power of the number of hammers a

consumer owns is far more predictive than the two other data points. I would be prepared to pay a relatively high price for data on hammer ownership. Now consider an alternative scenario where one additional data point is available: the number of nails a person uses per year. Let's assume that the general predictive power of nail consumption is almost as high as that of hammer ownership. The availability of nail consumption will have an effect on the price I am prepared to pay for the information on hammer ownership. (And if either bit of information is available to me alone, it is worth more to me. It's the basic law of supply and demand.)

In the next few years, the buying and selling of data will undoubtedly become a lot more streamlined, and companies will be able to pay for just the information they need. When that happens, the three market drivers described above will increasingly determine the price companies are willing to pay for information about their consumers.

Consumers, on the other hand, will get a much more transparent view of the value they are generating by allowing companies to collect data about them. Who knows, maybe they'll even be able to claim their share of the pie. It is not that far-fetched. After all, they are already getting loyalty discounts— lower prices on some items, frequent-flier miles, etc.—for sharing information about themselves. What could follow is that if they share even more, they could receive even more, such as cash back for everything they purchase after responding to a targeted ad.

PRIVACY AND THE VALUE EXCHANGE

The future looks great for the analytics community. Data is our fuel, and with zettabytes available, there is plenty for us to work with. There is, however, a big elephant in the room: privacy. And this is an elephant we can't ignore. It is a huge issue that will only grow in importance in the years ahead.

We opened the discussion of this issue in the introduction. Let's return to it here. And let me try to convince you that all the tracking we do can actually be a benefit to you. (And if I can't, let me say I am fully in favor of not disclosing any details about yourself if you don't want to.)

To see why having people tracking your behavior could be a benefit, let's go back to square one and start with all the free content—on television, on radio, online—that you and I enjoy. The free content isn't free, of course. It has to be paid for somehow. And usually that payment comes in the form of advertising. Let's look at television first (and just about everything we say here can be applied to radio as well) and then look at online.

People tell marketers all the time that there are too many commercials within their favorite TV programs. But I am willing to bet one of the reasons they feel that way is that a lot of the commercials they see have no relevancy in their lives. People in their thirties watching the network news are rarely a candidate for denture adhesives and folks in their seventies usually don't have any interest in sitting through an ad for the latest movie aimed at teens. Seeing stuff you don't care about is boring at best, and annoying at worst, and so it is no wonder that we complain about commercials.

But the more marketers know about you, the more they can deliver ads that will conceivably be of interest to you (and the more they can make sure you don't see commercials for things you don't care about). In fact, having more data means you will probably see fewer commercial messages, since advertisers will pay a premium for each one that reaches a targeted audience.

Some simple (and slightly oversimplified math) will prove the point. Let's say it costs $2 million to produce the typical half-hour sitcom, which runs 22 minutes. And let's assume advertisers pay $125,000 for each 30-second spot that appears within the show. Since there are 16 commercials available, advertising covers the complete cost of the show (and the networks and production companies make their profit when the show is repeated and/or syndicated).

That's the way it works now. But suppose advertisers could send their messages only to people who could benefit from what they have to offer (no feminine products pitches to men, for example). They could be willing to pay, say, $200,000 for each 30-second ad, meaning when you are watching *The Big Bang Theory* you would see only 10 commercials, not 16.

One of the industry's problems is that we haven't been able to explain clearly the economics. People often don't understand the relationship between advertising and the ability to watch television and surf the Internet for free. But the fact is, they are intertwined. And my position is that commercials and ads are inevitable since no one actually wants to pay the true cost of the media they consume. However, if marketers have data about me, at least they can make the messages I receive less intrusive.

But we haven't been able to communicate this idea very well. When the subject of targeting consumers comes up, the discussion quickly becomes all about privacy. And the same holds true when we talk to customers about the Internet. But, here again, people generally don't think about the economics. The Internet works economically because of the effectiveness of the online ads, and that effectiveness is driven by the data that is collected and used to personalize the messages. No data gathering, no effective ads, no free content.

The privacy issue is *hugely* important. And without context, it can seem creepy to know that people are tracking your every move when you shop or interact with digital communications.

I think two things will happen. One, government officials and our industry will probably reach a consensus to include certain regulations that will make it clear how we use all the information we collect. I think we are going to end up being totally transparent about it; and if you still don't like the idea, you will be able to opt out. (Of course, if you do, the amount and kinds of information you personally will be able to view for free will probably decrease, but you will be the one making that decision.)

I am not sure what the specifics of the final arrangement on privacy will be, but I think it will probably contain these components, which the industry has already agreed to:

1. Education: We will explain exactly how the tracking of consumer behavior works.

2. Our approach to transparency will call for multiple ways of disclosing and informing consumers about how we collect data and how we use it and let them opt out.

3. We will let consumers decide which data is collected and whether it can be shared with anyone else.

4. We will make sure—to the extent possible—that the data collected will be secure.

Here's one way the economics could work on the Internet. There might be "data walls," like the pay walls that exist on certain sites, such as the *Wall Street Journal*'s (wsj.com). If you go to that site, you can read the beginnings of most articles for free. To get the complete content, you need to sign up. Well, the same thing could happen at your favorite website. You would get limited access for free—and no information about you would be collected—but to have access to everything, you would have to agree to have data about you collected and used for targeting.

And then I do believe in a couple of years the privacy debate might fundamentally change. Whereas it is now very much about limiting the downsides of data collection, the focus in the future will be more on the advantages of having a well-detailed individual public profile and how companies can add a lot more value to our lives by knowing more about us.

This may sound Pollyannaish, but it is already happening. Millions of people allow Foursquare to capture real-time data about where they are geographically so they can get tips about things to explore in their immediate vicinity. Foursquare does not capture this data behind people's backs. They do it openly, and people agree to take part because they can see the value. Mint.com, now part of Intuit, has a value proposition that says: "You tell us your financial situation in detail, and we will give you advice to help improve it." Consumers find it so compelling, they eagerly provide their most intimate financial information so that Mint.com can help them optimize their personal finances.

Recommendation engines such as Amazon and Netflix are more widely known. They create value for the user—"if you bought/watched this, you will probably like that"—in exchange for personal information. All these firms have changed the game. They are not semi-secretly collecting data about individuals in the hope of not being found out. They aren't putting "opt out" clauses in fine print, hoping customers won't notice it (and opt out). They make data collection and value creation a central part of the value proposition, so that people actively want to participate.

My colleagues at Ogilvy Singapore came up with a very clever way to capture customer data for Pond's. The beauty care company has a skin care analyzer that people in a drugstore or at a cosmetic counter hold to four points on their face. The device then measures the composition, moisture, and oil rate of the skin. Based on this data, it determines the best Pond's product for the person's skin type. Customers are more than happy to submit their personal data to Pond's. The skin analyzer is the perfect data capture device.

Nike Plus is another great example. It is comprised of a kit that includes a sensor called an accelerometer (a fancy name for a motion sensor) that is placed in or on one of your shoes, and a receiver that attaches to your iPod Nano. The sensor detects each stride a runner takes and the information about speed and distance can be calculated. This way you are providing Nike with detailed personal information about your workouts. People don't mind since Nike uses that information to make their lives better. Obviously, you need to provide Nike with a lot of personal information to make this work.

In all these cases, consumers are voluntarily giving marketers information about themselves. I think the tracking of consumer behavior in all cases should be voluntary. If you don't want to disclose information about yourself, that should be your right. Just as it is the right of the people providing content to charge you for it, if you decide not to share details about yourself.

Even if you can't persuade consumers to hand over data, others might be able to. And they can always resell it to you with a customer's endorsement. This is already happening on Foursquare, where you will get a voucher or an offer from a restaurant or coffee shop because you are in the neighborhood.

It would be great if the privacy conversation would change

to one that stresses the potential value exchange, and as I said, I think it is going to happen. That's true in part because of the new generation of consumers. It always surprises me how little young people worry about privacy. They grew up on social networks. They are used to other people seeing their profiles and day-to-day actions. They openly broadcast their whereabouts to their friends and extended networks without hesitation.

TALENT CRUNCH

Statisticians are hot. Google claims they have the sexiest jobs in the world. IBM is hiring them by the thousands. They will have the pleasure to mine the enormous amounts of data that are being generated every day in our digital world. It's an unbelievable playground for mathematicians and statisticians, a place to find the insights that will drive the next innovations in medicine, new product development, finance, and, of course, marketing.

So where do we find these suddenly hot number crunchers? Good question. Here's the problem. Math and statistics are not exactly overwhelmingly popular among students, especially in the United States. According to the Organisation for Economic Co-operation and Development (OECD), which promotes policies to improve the economic and social well-being of people around the globe, US students rank thirty-fifth worldwide in math literacy. My own experience tells a similar story. Most of the résumés I receive are from people who learned their skills outside of the United States (mostly in China and India). Stricter visa regulations have made it harder to hire this talent. And even if I can, they don't always want to move. Increasingly, foreign mathematicians are less eager to leave the newfound prosperity of their countries of origin.

And it gets worse. Math skills alone are not enough. Math

marketers also need to have an affinity for marketing and a desire to work in what can be highly creative "right-brain" marketing environments where very few of their colleagues may understand, let alone know how to apply, math. Hence, math marketers must be able to use advanced mathematical techniques and explain their findings in a marketing context to a nontechnical audience. This is an extremely rare combination of skills.

BORDERLESS ECONOMY

As you know, the ease with which people can collaborate across time zones and borders has increased tremendously over the last few years. Not only basic email, but also more advanced collaboration platforms such as Basecamp, have made it possible for tasks to be performed remotely and for everyone around the world to learn faster and collaborate more effectively. These new collaboration platforms have the potential of turning the world into one big open marketplace where demand for skills (including analytics) will be matched to the supply of skills regardless of borders. This is already happening. Odesk.com is a perfect example of this.

When my colleague Colin Mitchell and I decided to write a blog, the doublethink that I mentioned earlier, our goal was to bring together the analytical and creative parts of the brain, which have traditionally been seen as opposites. We wanted it to be a blog where I would write the left brain column and Colin would write the right, and they would appear on the same screen simultaneously. It was a pretty basic idea, but we couldn't find any blogging software that had this approach as a template. So we needed a programmer who would create it, and since we were doing this as a side project, we needed to find someone who would not break the bank.

I googled "freelance programmers" and soon stumbled

upon Odesk, and a whole world I had not known of opened up. Odesk is a marketplace for talent. I described what I want to do and submitted a couple of visuals to give people an idea of what I wanted the blog to look like and asked if anyone was interested in doing the work.

I remember submitting my brief at 10 p.m. I never anticipated the response I got. The next morning I woke up to twenty-seven applications—from India, China, Thailand, Korea, Indonesia, Russia, Romania, Italy, Spain, Portugal, and Canada—for my little job. It was unbelievable. Every programmer had a detailed résumé on Odesk and included not only references, but hourly rates and test scores on technical tests organized by Odesk.

I needed a WordPress programmer, so I chose the programmer who had the highest scores on the WordPress test. He was also the fastest to complete the test (test timings were included). I got the entire site programmed and installed without a glitch in one week for $500. It was amazing.

Platforms like Odesk level the playing field for everyone. There are already a whole bunch of SPSS and SAS programmers, people who can deal with analytical software packages, available from Odesk. In the foreseeable future analytical talent will be available to everyone.

SPECIALIZATION

Analytic tools are evolving every day, which means an extremely high level of specialization is required to master them. This has caused an equally high degree of fragmentation in the math marketing world. Nobody is offering a complete range of analytical services and tools and, as a consequence, nobody provides the full 360-degree picture.

The grid below shows the skills I know my team needs— today.

BUSINESS PLANNING

Budget Setting and Allocation
Business Case Development
Scenario Planning

360 MEASUREMENT AND REPORTING

Performance Reporting
Dashboard Practice

ONLINE MEDIA ANALYTICS

Online Behavioral Targeting
Social Media Analytics
Online Media Analytics
Search Analytics

WEB ANALYTICS

Website Reporting
Site Testing and Optimization

TARGETING

Segmentation
Predictive Modeling

ECONOMETRIC MODELING

Campaign Performance Measurement
Marketing Mix Measurement
Media Mix Modeling

QUANTITATIVE RESEARCH

Tracking Studies
Online Research

Every box on this grid is getting more technical and more specialized. As a result, there will be the emergence of two types of analytics professionals. There will be specialists who will know everything about one or a handful of the boxes in the grid on page 231. Then there will be generalists, people who may have a degree of expertise in one area but also the ability to understand all the other flavors of analytics, which will enable them to orchestrate all specialties in a way that they can get the maximum value out of their data. If you want an easy analogy, think of medicine, where there are specialists and general practitioners. And just as in medicine—and all other technical fields—taking courses to keep up will be a must.

Ubiquitous Analytics

The technology industry is cyclical. Throughout history we have seen 15-to-20-year cycles where first a new technology (or technologies) is born, which then triggers a 10-year growth period where IT investments grow faster than the economy as a whole. This is usually followed by a period of reduced growth, during which new technologies get invented.

The last wave of tech innovation started in 1992, when the era of networked computers began, and probably ended in 2008. (For more background on technology cycles, see "Smart Computing Drives, The New Era of IT Growth," by Andrew H. Bartels—a Forrester Research report.)

We have now entered a new cycle of accelerated technology innovation and adoption. Some analysts refer to it as the era of smart computing. This is what IBM's Sam Palmisano was talking about when I quoted him in the introduction. We now live in an age when analytics and new computing models are part of everything we do, and their influence will only grow stronger.

TECHNICIANS AND MAGICIANS

If analytics is everywhere, will there still be room for imagination? That is a question I am often asked by our creative community. As mentioned throughout, I firmly believe that analytics and creativity are highly complementary. In fact, I believe it is the people who are doing the most basic analytic functions who are most in danger of losing their jobs. More and more of the analytical tasks will become automated, a trend that has already begun.

Early on I described how I went through the laborious task of trawling through log files to find out how consumers interacted with websites. Compare it to the examples of website optimization shown in Chapter 4. You can clearly see how a lot of the manual tasks are being automated.

In the future, fewer people will spend their days gathering and analyzing data. This will be done through highly automated tools and processes that are managed by a smaller army of technicians. They will tweak the systems so they can spit out more powerful insights more quickly.

But someone still has to take in all these insights and translate them into action. That's where creativity and intuitive decision making come into play. It's where the magic happens. So we will not only need the technicians, we'll also need the magicians. In the creative world of an advertising agency or marketing in general, these magicians will be a new breed of creatives with their senses open to insights coming from the technician's systems. They will use these insights to come up with new ideas that will transform a business.

Given the technical insights that will become available, there will be the need for a lot more magicians to make them work, and it will be crucial for technicians and magicians to work together closely.

ADAPT OR DIE

So how do you get your organization to learn from the insights you uncover? How do you become adaptable? This is something most companies struggle with. If the sexy little numbers suggest a change, will you be able to make that change? Or will you simply plow ahead for the next couple of years with the multimillion-dollar marketing campaign that has been planned. Companies that can become more agile will be the ones to benefit most from the power of analytics. Let's spend one more minute on that important point.

Most new products fail even when products are launched "successfully," because they usually aren't optimized. For example, some 50 percent of all software functionality is rarely or never used. That's a lot of wasted development effort. Inefficiencies are everywhere. A survey of US car manufacturers showed that their engineers on average spend only 20 percent of their time adding value. No wonder new product development teams everywhere have started to look at how they can do things differently.

More agile processes are drastically needed. One of the first to point that out was a group of software developers who got together in a ski resort in Utah in 2001 and drew up "The Agile Manifesto" in reaction to the traditional software development methods that prevailed at most companies, methods they deemed too rigid to deal with what was required to develop new software in the modern age. The principles of agile software development apply perfectly to marketing today. At its core, agile marketing is sensitive, adaptive, lean, fast, and iterative.

AGILE MARKETING IS

Sensitive	Keep yyour senses open to your customers. They define what value means for your organization.
Adaptive	Don't stick to outdated plans. Expect change and uncertainty and respond accordingly.
Lean	Eliminate waste by focusing relentlessly on the creation of value as defined by your customers.
Fast	Be quick without hurrying.
Interactive	Deliver today—adapt tomorrow. Test, observe, learn and iterate.

Agile marketing helps you become more adptable. It gives you the ability to act on the insights you derive from data. So how do we gather? Is there a system we can use to become more agile? I think there is, although it stems from an unlikely source—the military—more specifically, fighter pilot John Boyd.[*] A maverick with an aversion to authority (which didn't always work in his favor given his employer), Boyd was a superb pilot. His nickname was "40 Seconds" Boyd because he would bet any pilot $40 that, starting from a position of disadvantage, he could defeat them within 40 seconds in simulated dogfights. According to the legend, he never lost.

But Boyd was also an intellectual who studied the history and theory of warfare. He was one of the main architects behind the F-16, which was smaller and lighter than its predecessor, the F-15. It was the most agile plane of its time; and agility, as Boyd had shown, was crucial in aerial warfare.

After Boyd finished his work on the F-16, he devoted most of his time to developing a framework for agility which he called the OODA loop. OODA stands for:

---

[*]For more background on how Boyd's thinking applies to business, read the following *Fast Company* article: www.fastcompany.com/magazine159/pilot.html.

Observe

Orient

Decide

Act

To Boyd it was more than a simple summary of the steps human beings go through to make fast, seemingly intuitive decisions. He thought of it as a general framework for gaining competitive advantage. If you constantly run through your OODA loop, you can outmaneuver your competition.

Boyd's OODA loop is surprisingly applicable to achieving maximum agility in marketing. Let me show you what I mean.

Observe (and sense). Keep all your senses open, not just your eyes. In this digital world consumers are giving marketers constant cues about what they need and want. They have always done so but now marketers have the ability to capture these cues instantaneously because people live on platforms that generate data. We have a broad range of tools available that can capture and analyze all this data to get a pretty complete picture of what some have called "digital body language." Reading the digital body language and responding to it is what agile marketers do better than their competition.

Orient. The data from your observations needs to be processed to orient it for decision making by putting it in the context of what we already know about the customers and what we are trying to achieve with them.

Decide (and create). A fighter pilot's spectrum of potential decisions is pretty limited—up, down, left, right, faster, slower, shoot or don't—that's about it. (And, I suppose if things don't go well, "eject or not.")

In marketing, things are more complicated. We not only need to decide, we also have to create. The previous stage might identify content gaps or it might expose areas where we have content but not of the right quality. These issues need to be addressed in the creative process. What is different about how content is created in this agile system is how it is connected to the other stages in the loop. It is constantly informed by the information we are getting from our customers. That information not only gives new insights that can lead to new ideas; it also provides fast feedback on which ideas are working and which aren't. This feedback loop can change the creative process itself, making it more experimental and iterative. The agile principle of deliver today and adapt tomorrow can be applied to the creative process. Less time spent on planning and more on real time in market testing.

(Inter)act. The end goal is the customer interaction that drives value. These interactions can happen anywhere, anytime. The explosion of marketing channels has provided marketers with two crucial challenges: within-channel optimization and cross-channel integration.

Every time a new channel opens up—the next Twitter or Foursquare—marketers need to master it to ensure the interactions are happening in the most optimal way. The second challenge is cross-channel integration. How can you make sure that all touch points are synchronized in a way that ensures a consistent customer experience across every channel? This is where marketing automation platforms can play a vital role in managing the complexity of all customer touch points.

PREPARING FOR THE FUTURE

If the future plays out the way I think it will, there are a number of steps you can take to be ready.

1. *Become (and remain) data literate.* There will be no place to hide. Everyone will need to have a grounding in what data can do for them. Without a basic level of data literacy you will simply be left behind. (You will also miss out on all the fun and the excitement that the data-driven world has to offer.)

   The good news, if you have read this far, is that you can call yourself data literate. That's what this book is all about. You have learned how to segment your customers based on their current value and even how to predict their future behavior using advanced statistical techniques. You have seen how you can really get to understand their needs and the attitudes that drive their behavior. We taught you how to find your targets in the most effective way, be it by geography, in media, and or on digital networks. You know how to measure what works and what doesn't, and you know how to optimize your efforts using advanced techniques. And you should also know how to determine how much to spend on driving demand.

   That's all good. But the world will keep evolving, and you will need to keep up. Knowing everything there is to know about VCRs when the world has switched to DVRs doesn't help you much.

2. *Focus on what you want to achieve.* Given your newfound excitement about all the possibilities data can give you, you are at risk of falling into a common trap. You may start thinking about everything data *can* do as opposed to pondering what it *should* do for you. My point? Don't get lost in the endless

possibilities. You need to focus on how you can get the maximum return out of these possibilities. This is exactly why this book was structured the way it was. Every chapter focused on questions business people deal with daily. This is where you should start as well. What are the decisions you are taking today where you feel you can use the power of the sexy little numbers.

3. *Find skills—build or buy.* All the math marketing in the world won't do a bit of good unless your company is organized to employ it. People—not numbers, not algorithms—make the difference in successful math marketing. To get this right without the expense or dislocation caused by organizational turmoil, set up a base of skills, construct a center of excellence (COE; more on this in a minute), forge the right external partnerships, and foster a pervasive math marketing culture.

CENTER OF EXCELLENCE

A question many people ask me is how they can get started with introducing analytics into their organizations. Many companies nurture advanced analytic skills within their organization by establishing a center of excellence (COE) for math marketing. This group usually resides within a marketing intelligence group that, in turn, often sits within a broader strategy group.

If you go this route—and if your company is big enough, I believe it makes sense—your COE must consist of at least one web analyst (who looks at how much traffic you are generating and from where), a website optimizer (this would be the person in charge of multivariate testing and the like), a social metrics expert (someone who is tracking what is happening on the Web 2.0), a database marketer (a generalist who links the data with the marketers), a search analyst (a search engine optimizer), a quantitative market analyst, a qualitative market researcher, a media analyst, a digital media analytics expert, an audience researcher, an econometrician, a data miner, and a PR measurement specialist.

But since few companies can sustain an internal COE with such a degree of specialization, many of them look outside for partners who bring some, if not most, of these capabilities. If you can afford to do only one job internally, I would hire a search analyst, someone who can make sure your company's name and product pop up when a customer is looking on the web for something you do.

External Partnerships. The role of external partners will only grow larger as math marketing evolves. Companies eager to acquire math marketing by way of outsourcing need to establish the right organizational framework to support these relationships; that means they have to make sure everyone in the company is receptive to what analytics can do. On the other side, the ideal math marketing partner of the future will need to be strong across two dimensions:

- *Broad aperture*: They must comprehend the marketing landscape in its entirety, understanding all media and all elements of the marketing mix. They must be able to link the analytics activities to the business issues you are trying to resolve.

- *Specialty skills*: Math marketers must have all the skills necessary to master the modern math marketing toolkit. Within that toolkit you'll find econometric modeling, data mining, statistics, web analytics, online advertising serving competencies, quantitative market research techniques, dashboard and visualization technologies, search engine optimization, and social media analytics. In addition, of course, math marketers will need to keep up with the latest developments.

One reason I think we see a huge number of partnerships is that there is clearly no one place you can go to get everything you need. The current math marketing landscape is lacking a clear top dog.

ACKNOWLEDGMENTS

I wouldn't have been able to write this book without the help and inspiration from the people I have had the pleasure to interact with over the years. First of all, I want to thank Miles Young for asking me to write this book and supporting me throughout, and Colin Mitchell for convincing me I could write it. It was the amazing work of the analytics team at Ogilvy that gave me the material for this book. I would like to specifically thank Deborah Balme, Jorge Ruiz, and Leon Shim for their help, and David Coppock and Jim Dravillas, both among the most original analytical thinkers I have ever had the pleasure to work with. Without their ideas, writing this book would have been a lot harder.

I also owe an incredible amount of gratitude to the people who helped me at the beginning of my career. Philippe Naert for showing me twenty years ago there was a career in marketing analytics. Jan Vanaken and Philip Greenfield for hiring me in Brussels. Ira Helf and Patty Lyon for mentoring me in my early years at Ogilvy and for giving me the opportunities to live in London, San Francisco, and New York. Brian Fetherstonhaugh and Gunther Schumacher for continuing to believe in me, and Carla Hendra for putting analytics front and center at Ogilvy and for giving the small-town kid from Belgium a shot. Thank you, Ben Richards, for coming up with the title for this book after a couple of beers in the Landmark Tavern. I also want to thank Jeremy Katz for being the driving force and inspiration throughout this entire process, Paul B. Brown, who made me feel like we had been working together for years from our first meeting on, and John Mahaney, who taught me the real meaning of the word "thorough."

Most important, I would like to thank my family. My mom and dad, who I wish I could see more often. They always gave me the freedom to do what I wanted but somehow kept me focused and disciplined. And finally, my wife, Katherine, who, while I was writing this book, put her career on hold and gave birth to our two lovely children. Without her I'd be a shadow of the person I am today.

INDEX

Page numbers of graphs and charts appear in italics.